RANKING
SECRETS

THE UNDERGROUND PLAYBOOK FOR GENERATING
UNLIMITED TRAFFIC, LEADS & SALES WITHOUT
SPENDING A DIME ON PAID ADS

ROBERT KANAAT

ISBN-13: 979-8643351726

TABLE OF CONTENTS

THANK YOU

Thank you so very much for your purchase. As a **FREE GIFT**, I want to give you access to my *SEO Consumer Awareness Guide*.

In it, I reveal powerful, behind-the-scenes secrets that SEO agencies use to earn your trust and how to properly vet them to make sure you're getting real value.

Here's exactly what you'll discover in that hard-hitting guide:

- 8 common mistakes to avoid when choosing an SEO company

- 7 questions to ask before ever giving an SEO consultant access credentials to your website

- 6 costly misconceptions about SEO

- 5 technical factors that can destroy your ability to

rank

- 4 red flags that your SEO firm is going to rip you off

- 3 tactics that every SEO strategy should employ

- 2 most powerful principles in SEO

- The importance of value over price

To claim your FREE copy of the *SEO Consumer Awareness Guide* just head to https://outrankfast.com/free-guide

INTRODUCTION

Search Engine Optimization (SEO) is the Holy Grail of marketing. It's pursued, sought after and chased by hundreds of millions of businesses vying for attention across the world. But let's face it. There's a reason why it's so alluring. It's free. Organic. And highly relevant.

When you appear at the top of a keyword search, it's like winning the lottery. Increased visibility results in a natural rise in relevancy. And when you're relevant, people instantly trust you and buy whatever it is that you're selling.

But on the flipside, we also know that SEO is hard. No, scratch that. It can often seem downright impossible to rank for certain keywords. So what gives? Why's it so difficult? And why is that no matter what you seem to do, you can't claw your way to the top?

Questions like this are common. Everyone knows that it's brutally challenging to rank for the most competitive keywords. After all, there are only 10 spots on the first page.

Just ten lonely little spots. And, let's face it, the first page is where you absolutely need to be.

Why? Because, just about no one is going past that first page. Roughly 9 out of 10 never move to the second page in a search. More importantly, a lion's share of the traffic on that first page go to the top 3 results, receiving a whopping 61.5% of all clicks.

Clearly, if Google deems you relevant, especially on a high-volume keyword, and you somehow snag one of those illustrious top-few spots, you're in the money. But how do you get there? What determines who wins and who loses?

Okay, the answer to that question isn't simple. In fact, it's fairly complex with hundreds of factors that are weighted in the overall algorithm. But that doesn't mean it's impossible to understand. It's not. And, as you read this book, you'll come to realize that, with the right approach, it is achievable.

However, don't expect it to happen overnight. Nor should you expect it to happen right away. The truth is that many people who approach SEO end up in a state of frustration for one reason. They expect instantaneous results. After all, we live in a society where we have on-demand everything.

Why should we have to wait weeks, months, and sometimes even years, just to achieve our goal of ranking at the top of a keyword search? With a mindset like that, it's clear to see why people end up in frustration. Yet, I know that it's different for you.

For you to pick up a book like this means one thing and one thing only. You're willing to invest your time and energy into learning, understanding and practicing the art of authentic SEO. And to discover just what it takes to outrank and literally dominate your competition on any search.

The truth is that success in any field requires hard work and discipline. And in SEO it ultimately equates to a willingness to do the most amount of work for the least initial return. And not trying to do the least amount of work for the biggest return.

Once you have that mindset, you can achieve all of your ranking dreams. No, it will not happen right away. But what you'll learn in this book will be the long-term strategies and tactics that have helped me generate tens of millions of unique visitors without spending a dime on paid ads.

So, what is SEO at the end of the day? And what does it take to succeed? At its core, there is one simple concept that you must understand. And that is trust. Google's trust, to be more specific. When you can get Google to trust you implicitly, that is when you will win this game called SEO.

Break Google's trust, and watch as your rank drops faster than a ship's anchor. Seems like a simple concept, doesn't it? Just get Google to trust you and you're all set. But you know just as much as the next person that gaining that trust isn't simple and it doesn't happen quickly.

Yet, once you come to understand just what it takes to get Google to trust you, the pathway forward is clear. There are specific steps you need to take to build that trust over time. No, it doesn't happen quickly. But there are ways to ethically speed things up

SECRET 1
THE CORE FOUNDATION OF RANK

No. This can't be happening.

I slowly ran my fingers through my hair as I repeated those words over and over in my mind. Staring blankly over an epic landscape of towering steel and glass skyscrapers, I played out all the worst-case-scenarios in my mind.

How could this happen?

I shivered. Goosebumps. Teeth chattering. Trembling, I felt helpless. Lost. Spinning out of control. Hurtling towards my impending doom. I wondered what, if anything, I could do.

My main traffic source was just pulled. The same traffic source I'd spent tens of thousands of dollars investing in was no longer available to me. A traffic source that produced a gold mine of high-end, buyer-hungry leads was gone. Like a cloud of smoke. Poof. It vanished into thin air.

Those leads were a critical part of my business. I needed them. Without them, I was as good as done. Without leads, how could I make sales? How could I pay my staff? And how could I possibly stay afloat? It was impossible.

Long before I knew much about marketing, I'd hit my proverbial iceberg. And like the Titanic, I was sinking fast. It was only a matter of time. The ship was taking on water and the bow was rising, about to plunge into an icy sea of abyss.

I was out of options and devoid of solutions. With nowhere left to turn, I wondered how it would all play out. It's a period of my life I'd rather forget. I teetered on the brink. Pain. Turmoil. Endless stress and anxiety hijacked my mind.

I thought the unthinkable.

How could I make this pain just stop?

That was the governing thought running through my mind. Thinking about ways I could end it all. Escape. Run. Fold like the deck of cards my life and my business had become.

I knew I needed to do something. And fast. So I scrambled. How could I drive traffic to my business? Where could I find the same, highly targeted, buyer-hungry leads I had paid so dearly for? But this time, without a budget?

It was early in the days of search engines like Google. But even then, I reluctantly realized the power they held. I knew that countless millions of searches were happening every single second of every single day. All I needed was a fraction of a percentage of that.

But the problem was this. I hadn't invested in optimizing my site for Google. I'd relied on a single paid traffic source for leads and sales. That was it. It was the nail in my proverbial coffin. I'd put all my eggs into one basket. And as a result, I was resigned to my own demise.

I needed to pivot. But it was too late in the game. How could I drive targeted organic traffic, fast? And how could I find the right type of customers who could afford what I was selling? I didn't have months or years. I had days. Maybe weeks.

It was too little too late. As hard as I tried to learn and optimize on my own, I simply ran out of time. The business crashed and that deck of cards I had built came falling down. The ensuing pain cut deep. I was left hopeless. Penniless. I felt like a total and complete failure.

My life was spinning out of control in a state of chaos. Yet, it was this very experience that led me to dig deep. It sent me on a journey of discovery. To understand the fundamental principles for driving targeted, organic traffic in droves.

I also came to the realization that I was building my business the wrong way. I was relying on a single source of traffic. And I was also ignoring many of the fundamental aspects of marketing. The deeper I went, the more I realized I didn't know.

There seemed to be so much information out there that it sent me off into a million different directions. But that journey led to an inherent understanding of sales and organic marketing on a deeper, more profound level than I ever had before.

Although it was too little too late to save the sinking Titanic that was my business, something else happened. I became an expert in an industry known for creating confusion. I discovered the foundational building blocks of search algorithms and it all began making sense to me.

But this all came at a high price. Time. The most valuable

commodity we all have. I was too thick-headed to ask for help. So I stubbornly went on this journey alone. Mistake after mistake, I refused to relent. I refused to give up and throw in the towel.

The knowledge I learned during that period saved me. It allowed me to launch a popular blog called, Wanderlust Worker where I share everything about goal setting, habits and failure. In building that site, I learned precisely how to craft killer content that ranks.

I repeatedly prodded and tested my ranking secrets in the real world. That gave me the ammunition I needed to know precisely how to create rapid-fire success without spending a dime on paid ads. And most importantly, I discovered how to get attention in a noisy world.

I soon realized that this information was invaluable. But I also realized that most of what others teach about ranking was wrong. There is so much misinformation and disinformation that most people don't know where to turn.

That's precisely one of the reasons why I knew I had to write this book. To convey to you everything I've learned over the years. To pull back the proverbial curtain. To reveal the mechanics behind search. And to share the secrets to ranking on search engines like Google and YouTube.

Had I known then what I know now, my business might have survived. It might have even thrived. Instead, it crashed and burned. Failed. Collapsed. And it left me staggering to pick up the million little broken pieces.

But we can't go back in time, right? And I wouldn't want to. The lessons I've learned from that experience have shown me what's possible in the field of organic search. It's not just about ranking content. This is about getting your offers in front of relevant audiences that are ready to buy whatever you're peddling.

WHO DO YOU TRUST?

I was a ball of nerves. Sweating profusely, I slipped my finger into the collar of my shirt. I could feel it dripping alongside the back of my neck like raindrops cascading down a pane of glass. I was drenched.

How could I be this nervous?

The last time I spoke in front of a group of people was in high school speech class. It was my biggest fear. My introverted mind raced with a million thoughts a minute. How would they judge me? What would they think of me?

I looked over at my mentors who were busy speaking to the group. Nervously waiting, I watched them in anticipation. It was like an old silent movie playing in black and white. Their mouths were moving, but no sound was coming out.

Ears ringing, I could feel my pulse in the back of my throat. Gulp. I swallowed hard as the tension built. My heart thumping louder and louder by the moment. Thump, thump, thump. *Could they hear it too?*

Dean Graziosi and Joe Polish were about to introduce me to a small group of entrepreneurs who'd paid $100,000 each to be in that room. I didn't take that lightly at all.

Robert are you ready? asked Dean.

Am I ready? Are you kidding me? I'm a ball of nerves. I'm falling apart. Can't you see what I'm going through!

No. I needed to be calm. Cool. Collected. My eyes darted at the two marketing legends. Slowly, I rose from my chair. You could easily hear a pin drop in that room. It was all eyes on me.

Joe and Dean looked on, sensing my nerves. I felt faint. *You can do this,* I said waveringly to myself in my mind.

But I wasn't convinced. I felt underprepared. That last minute hasty decision to ditch my presentation and just wing it was a huge mistake. But there was no turning back now. It's was game time.

Making my way to the front of the room, I quivered as I looked around at titans in business. I felt unmatched. Unqualified.

I shouldn't be here. I'm nobody.

I stood motionless. Expressionless. Frozen, waiting for my cue. All eyes were on me. I gulped down hard.

Fear gripped and the sweat rose off my palms in sheets as Dean launched into an introduction, showering me with praise and gratitude for all I had done for him.

The crazy thing is that I didn't feel like I'd done much.

I'd helped write a few articles in *Forbes* and *Entrepreneur Magazine* to promote his new book, *Millionaire Success Habits*. But to him, that was a big deal.

On the phone, when he invited me to that mastermind, I remember how excited I was. I had to fly 7,000 miles just to be in that room, but I didn't care. It might as well have been 70,000 miles.

But right then, right there, all of that faded away. A distant memory. The excitement melted like ice cream on a hot summer's day. And it was replaced by pure, unadulterated fear.

I fumbled for words as Dean passed the virtual baton to me. He could see I was struggling. I stuttered. Stammered. Paused. And when I spoke, my voice was shaky.

I looked out at the crowd who stared intently at me. I grasped for something. Anything. That's when Dean jumped in to save the day. He lobbed question after question at me.

Eventually, I loosened up. *You've got this,* I said to myself. And I did. I was in state. Flowing. I was dropping gold nuggets left and right. I dove into the fundamental principles of what it takes to rank. And I had their complete, undivided attention.

It was a rush. But I don't tell you this to impress you. I say it to impress upon you the importance of trust. What's far more important and relevant is how I ended up in that room with those people.

Just months earlier I was living in obscurity. In the wake of another failed attempt at business. I'd given up. I was fed up. Defeated. I'd thrown in the proverbial towel again.

That's when I made a decision. It was the product of a

mental shift. I was reminded of something Tony Robbins said. *Success leaves clues. If you want to succeed, find someone who's already succeeding, and model their behavior.*

But I needed a hook. A way to get their attention. Luckily, I was writing for *Forbes* and *Entrepreneur Magazine* at the time. So I hatched a plan and started my outreach. I would interview highly successful entrepreneurs to learn their stories. Then write about them in major publications.

I combined it with the added benefit of ranking for a major keyword. Because, after all, those publications carry a lot of weight and authority on the internet. And ranking for big keywords was far easier when you have carte blanche on big media domains.

So I reached out to people who were highly successful. People like Russell Brunson and Ryan Deiss. I wanted to learn straight from the masters.

I moved from working tirelessly to help myself, to instead helping others. I had no expectations of anything in return. But what I didn't realize was the sheer power of the principle of reciprocity.

I wrote about Russell Brunson, the founder of ClickFunnels, the fastest growing SaaS company in the world. And, the legendary Ryan Deiss, an icon in the online marketing industry. Both are brilliant minds. World-class copywriters. And epic direct response marketers.

The conversation with Deiss was pivotal.

I'd love to introduce you to my business partner, Roland Frasier.

Who? I asked.

I had no idea who he was. But I graciously accepted. After all, this was Ryan Deiss. An absolute legend. But the truth is that I had no clue who Frasier was. I had no idea how much influence he had in the industry.

Nor did I know just how well connected he was to the people that I idolized in the space. People like Frank Kern, Dean Graziosi, John Assaraf and many others.

You see, here's what happened. Hoping to build his personal brand, Frasier asked if I'd be willing to write about him. I graciously accepted. But on one condition. He had to introduce me to all the influential people he knew.

Sure! Of course! I can do that, he said vehemently.

Little did I know that this one conversation could open doors that I never knew could be opened. After doing a piece on Frasier in Forbes, I was swiftly introduced to the "players" in the marketing field. I met Jason Fladlien, the $100 million webinar king, who bent over backwards to help me create my webinar.

I met Dean Graziosi and Joe Polish. And that's precisely how I wound up speaking at the Genius $100K Group. I still vividly recall the conversation with Graziosi just after Frasier introduced me.

You came through Roland? You must have done something to impress him. How can I help you?

Here was one of the most brilliant marketers on the planet asking how he could help me. Seriously? My only thought was this.

Who are you, Roland Frasier?

All of these successful entrepreneurs were just one phone call away for Frasier. Literally. The reason this story is important to the concept of Google's trust is because the innerworkings of SEO is founded on the same basic principles that make the business world go round.

When someone you trust introduces you to someone else whom they also trust, there's an instant bond that's formed. That bond is based on the chain of trust. Think about it this way. How do you usually find a good doctor or dentist or *chiropractor*, or any other service provider?

Sure, some people go online and they search for one. They check all the reviews and do extensive due diligence. But others call their friends. They'll say something like, *Hey, is the dentist you go to any good?* or, *Who's your doctor and how long have you known him?* or *Who's your personal trainer? Have you gotten results with her?*

These questions are rooted in the foundational aspect of trust. It is, and will always be, a cornerstone in our society. Google knows this. They understand that trust supersedes everything in the real world. And it's also an integral part of the digital world.

The basic premise is this. If you've personally dealt with someone and you implicitly trust them, that trust can be conveyed to someone else. It can also be conveyed to groups of people. This concept interlaces your ability to rank for anything.

Trust is also the reason why I wound up speaking at the $100K group to titans in business. I helped Deiss. Then Frasier. That created reciprocity and a chain of trust that extended to others. And that's precisely what allowed me to be in that room sharing the top strategies for dominating SEO in any industry or niche.

All because of the conveyance of trust.

Trust is a core concept in SEO. A foundational secret. You have to respect and pay homage to it. But it takes time to build trust. We all know that.

21

In the real world, it takes months or years of knowing someone and interacting with them before you can truly trust them. Yet, it can also be sped up. When someone you already trust vouches for someone else, it creates a bridge of trust.

That's how it works. We rely on the experience of others and their relationships to base our personal level of trust in anyone or anything. Sure, we read reviews and also do our own research online. That all plays into the trust equation.

However, there's nothing that instills more trust than knowing a person very well who already trusts another person. It puts your mind at ease. You worry less and become more confident in the decision to engage the services of a stranger when it comes through your personal network.

Think about this. What happens when your best friend for over a decade refers you to her doctor? Do you bother to check reviews? Or do you take her word for it? For most, that's more than enough. Why? Because that bridge of trust supersedes all else.

Imagine I'd reached out to Brunson or Deiss without carrying the weight of a highly trusted media publication. Would I get their attention? Likely not. Unless I was a big influencer or we had a mutual trusted connection, my messages would likely go unnoticed.

But I came from the angle of Forbes and Entrepreneur Magazine. Two very trusted names in the media space. Who doesn't want to be featured or written up about there? As a writer for those publications, there was a sincere chain of trust.

In fact, this core concept of trust shapes every interaction we have in life and in business. Why do you think credit scores are so important? When you have a perfect FICO credit score of 850 here in the United States, lenders will literally throw money at you.

Why? Just because a little score tells them it's okay to do that? That score encompasses so much. It tells a creditor how trustworthy an individual is to borrow money. That's possible due to the recorded history of trust in transactions.

Do they pay their credit cards, loans, and other notes on time? How much debt are they carrying? What's their income? What's the debt-to-income ratio? All of these factors play into a credit score's computational algorithms.

It's no different in the SEO world. In fact, Google has taken the principles of the real world and shrunken them down into this microcosm called the internet. And, it's largely based its algorithms on these very foundational understandings of trust.

However, in the SEO world, the currency works a bit differently. Rather than payments and debt, there's content and authority. Here, trust isn't broken when you miss a payment. Rather, it's broken when you try to employ sneaky tactics to rank faster.

For example, if you try to build out thousands of low-quality links using software or by hiring vendors online, Google knows you're cheating. How? It knows organic content and linking from paid spammy bots and link exchanges. If you try to game the system, you could be in for a world of hurt.

Think about it this way. In the world of credit scores, it's hard to get a credit card with little credit history. If you have less than 2 years of credit history, banks are reluctant to lend you money. Securing a loan or a credit card is incredibly hard. Especially without a high down payment, an exorbitant interest rate or a co-signer.

Keep in mind that there's a risk profile here. Banks understand that and they factor that into their calculations. It's clear to see how trust weighs into every decision in the real world. Every exchange, interaction, and agreement is rooted in a level of trust.

It's no different in the SEO world. And today, Google no longer trusts websites implicitly. Especially newcomers. Registering a brand-new domain and expecting to rank right away is like trying to get a huge loan with little to no credit history. It just won't happen. So don't expect it to.

Yes, the explanations run far deeper than that. What constitutes trust at the end of the day involves so many factors. But so do credit scores. I use the analogy because it's the simplest way you can understand the first foundational secret to how SEO works.

It's all based on trust.

However, the problem today is that most people don't want to wait months or years to build trust. Just like we don't want to wait years to build a credit score before applying for a car loan, a credit card or a mortgage. Are there ways to speed things up? Yes. But not by much.

In the SEO world, trust is built slowly and broken quickly. However, by getting other people that Google already trusts, to trust you, that speed can increase. That's why links on big media sites are so coveted. They're trusted names in the online world and those links carry weight.

It's not easy to get those links. Google knows that. But these links create a chain of trust. And when Google trusts you, your chances for appearing relevantly in any search skyrockets. And that right there is the name of game.

REPAIRING TRUST

I had a best friend in high school. Alex. We were inseparable. Nearly everything we did away from school, we did it together. Travel. Coffee. Hanging out with friends. Studying. And spending every waking moment dreaming big.

As high school finished, we both went our separate ways. I went to college at NYU, while he stayed back in Los Angeles and attended a community college. After college, I moved back to LA to study law. I wanted to be a lawyer. Or so I thought.

But law bored me and I quickly lost interest. I wanted to make money. And I wanted to do it fast. I knew there was only one option forward. I needed to start a business. So, my best friend, Alex, and I, went into business together.

We were both wild-eyed and naive to the business world. We had no idea what it took to succeed. We just knew we wanted it badly. But after working for years, things fell apart. We were forced to fire all the staff because we ran out of money.

The hard part was that we just gave up. And like any two friends who go into business together, we had a big falling out. The trust was gone. Vanished. Disappeared. I went into business with someone else and he was hurt. So hurt that he wanted to find any way he could to get back at me.

I haven't seen Alex in 10 years. However, I'd never go into business with him again. And, I doubt he would go into business with me. We lost trust in one another. Repairing that trust is incredibly hard. How do you go back and reverse all the damage that was done?

Or, how about in a romantic relationship, when one catches the other cheating. How do they repair that trust once it's broken? How do they go back to the way things used to be? You just can't. How about when you file for bankruptcy? Why does it take so long for creditors to trust you again?

You see, when you lose someone's trust (anyone's trust), reversing and repairing the damage is difficult. Sometimes it's downright impossible. I want you to look at SEO the same way. Trying to go back after you've broken the rules to regain Google's trust is incredibly hard.

In fact, some would also claim that this is impossible. Of course, it depends on just how deeply that trust was violated or broken. For some people, there are things others do that feel impossible to recover from. That applies as much in the real world as it does in the digital world.

Can trust be repaired? Sure. It's possible. With the right amount of time and effort, anything can happen. But it won't happen quickly by any means. And if you violate someone's trust, don't expect for things to be cheeky or rosy right away.

In the SEO world, Google acts the same way. Cross them by creating low-quality, spammy links, and you'll suffer. Spin or duplicate content, and you'll face their wrath. The problem is, most of the time, you won't even know it.

They won't call you and tell you how disappointed they are in you. They won't email you and tell you that you'll no longer appear in their search results. Nope. Almost never. You'll just be shadowbanned. And you'll be forced to scratch your head wondering what happened.

Sometimes, when the trust is so severely broken, there's a manual penalty incurred. They will literally manually remove your domain from their search indexes. Other times, your fate will simply be tied to another algorithm adjustment.

Sure, you can recover at times. You can use tools, for example, to disavow bad links. However, the disavow tool is meant for advanced SEOs who know what they're doing. If you're a beginner or a novice, don't attempt to disavow links. It could do more damage than good.

The reason why I talk about repairing trust is so that you understand the importance of not violating Google's trust in the first place. When you stay on the straight and narrow, and you ensure that the things you do are above board, it's your surest way to so-called SEO glory.

Keep in mind that millions of people are competing for the same lucrative spots. There's true scarcity here. Page one only has 10 listings on Google. And that's certainly where you want to be. And those top 3 spots? They get the lion's share of clicks. 62.5% to be exact.

So if you try to cheat, use link-building bots or start

spinning out low-quality content, you'll struggle to gain any traction. You won't rank. You'll wallow away in obscurity. There's so much competition that you'd be kicking yourself by trying to take shortcuts that don't exist.

We'll dive into more detail on this later. For now, try to stay on Google's good side. Don't bend or break the rules. Build trust bridges. Don't build walls that will destroy your chances of making progress and climbing those illustrious Search Engine Results Pages (SERPs).

SECRET 2
HONING YOUR SKILLS

I need this job.

That's all I could think about. Just two weeks earlier, I'd dropped out of law school. And with it, my mother's hopes and dreams for me becoming a lawyer.

But I was desperate. I needed money. And law school wasn't paying me. After 4 years of undergrad, I was sick of school. Fed up. Tired of struggling. Tired of not having money to pay my bills. It was a brash decision. But it was now or never.

I still remember the look on the dean's face when I dropped out. I remember how she crinkled her nose and pursed her lips. She tried hard not to show her cards. But It was clear. Her gaze was familiar. That look of disappointment was painted all over her face.

Are you sure you want to do this?

I remember the look in her eyes when she said it. A look of concern, like are you all right? No. I wasn't all right. I was broke. And I needed to make money.

Yes. I am sure, I said, vehemently. And I was sure. I was positive, in fact. Nothing had been clearer to me.

As I sat there in that room waiting for the interviewer to show up, all those thoughts flooded my mind. And all the self-doubt crept in. My nerves were fried. I was desperate.

I shifted. Side to side. Then again. Palms sweating. I waited for someone to walk in, but those minutes felt like hours. Eventually, I heard her. The clacking of heels in the hallway. The shuffling of papers in her hand.

She strode in confidently. Business attire. Her blonde hair perched in a ponytail, she beamed a smile, sat down and introduced herself.

Hi. I'm Jill. I'm in charge of the marketing department here. It's great to meet you.

It wasn't just anyone interviewing me. This was the head of the marketing department. Oh God, I thought. But her pale blue eyes put me at ease. She set down her notepad and papers and got organized. Pen at the ready, she quickly lobbed questions at me.

The niceties were over. It was game time. Her beaming smile turned into a serious crowing of her brow as she asked me questions and jotted down my answers. I wasn't the first person she'd interviewed that day. And she made me well aware of that.

How do websites work? She asked. It was such a general question, but it needed a specific response. *And what makes you think you can manage one at a professional level? A corporate level?*

Sure. I didn't have the experience. Not on paper at least.

But I was right for the job. I just knew it. All I needed to do was convince the middle-aged marketing manager in front of me of that.

I knew that technical talk would get me nowhere fast. I needed to explain the importance of writing good, clean code. But how could I make it relatable? How could I make it so that someone non-technical could understand it?

Look, I said. Imagine it this way. When you build a house, you pour a concrete foundation. That foundation has to be firm to support the structure. If the foundation is too shallow, the home will collapse. The foundation is so important, that when tall buildings are built, the foundations can run hundreds of feet into the ground. The problem is, to the naked eye, you can't see that.

But master builders understand this. They make sure the foundation runs deep enough to support the structure sitting on top of it. But not only that, they're required to take so many other factors into account. They need an architect to draft the plans and create blueprints, collaborate with the trades, work with inspectors, and more.

They understand the entire process from start to finish. And they know how to systemize, automate and coordinate that build. The same thing applies for websites. A good website needs a solid codebase. Think about it like that concrete foundation. It also needs structural framing, like the walls, floors, ceilings, windows and doors. That's like the HTML. And to top it off, it needs to look pretty through the proper use of CSS and other design elements.

Her eyes widened. And a few minutes in, I knew she was sold. I had taken a complex concept and broken it down into simple terms. I made it relatable. Understandable. Easier to digest and grasp. I left the interview with my spirits soaring.

It was my first job interview and I'd nailed it (no pun intended). It was then, right there, that I realized the importance of simplicity. To make concepts easy to understand and digest for people is crucial. And today, that's precisely what Google wants.

While using obscure or academic words is good sometimes, based on the topic, Google knows that the majority of its users want content that's easy to consume. It wants you to break it down so that it's understandable for most people.

It should solve a problem in an easy-to-explain way. This is definitely easier said than done. The truth is that it's hard to break complex concepts down into something that's easy to digest. It's hard to make your content flow and interweave stories to keep people engaged.

But that's precisely what you have to get good at doing. Look, this is not a writing contest. You don't need to become a master wordsmith. You just need to make concepts simple and relatable. You don't need to get all scientific or write some dissertation.

However, you certainly should be an expert. Expertise is a requirement. If you're not an expert, become one in your niche. It won't happen overnight. Then again, nor will number one rankings for the most competitive search terms.

You see this in the SEO field all the time. There are plenty of people screaming from the mountain tops, claiming to be experts, but how many people are actually able to generate millions of unique organic visitors per year? How many people have truly mastered the principles of SEO?

Today, as someone who's grown my blog, wanderlustworker.com, into a traffic-generating machine, receiving millions of organic visitors per year, I can tell you firsthand what it takes to dominate the SEO space. And to do it the right way.

The truth is that SEO is hard. But so is paid advertising. Unless your messaging is truly on point, and you really know how to address the pain of your audience, then you'll likely fall flat with paid ads. And for good reason. No one has an unlimited budget.

There's a reason why SEO is one of the best investments you can make when it comes to marketing your business. According to The Direct Marketing Association, every dollar you spend with SEO can earn you roughly $22.24 back. That outpaces both display and keyword ads.

But the beauty of SEO is that you don't have to continue spending forever. Once you rank, oftentimes, it's fairly sticky. For example, I have content that's ranked number one on Google for years in a row. Once you understand exactly how to do it, it's a no-brainer to invest in SEO.

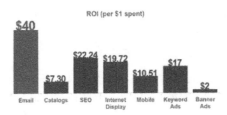

Source: *The Direct Marketing Association*

But like others, you're probably wondering where to begin. You've probably been running around in what my friend, David Sharpe, calls the guru gauntlet. There's just so much information overload that most people don't know where to start.

The reason why I started out by talking about the

concept of trust is because most people like to complicate SEO. They talk about *On-Site This*, *Off-Page That*, and algorithm adjustments, trying to come across as highly knowledgeable when at the end of the day it really all boils down to trust.

I recently read a book by Gary Keller who opened my eyes to the simplicity of what it takes to succeed. If you haven't read it, I'd highly suggest picking it up. In that book entitled, *The One Thing: The Surprisingly Simple Truth Behind Extraordinary Results*, Keller says:

When you want the absolute best chance to succeed at anything you want, your approach should always be the same. Go small.

"Going small" is ignoring all the things you could do and doing what you should do. It's recognizing that not all things matter equally and finding the things that matter most. It's a tighter way to connect what you do with what you want. It's realizing that extraordinary results are directly determined by how narrow you can make your focus.

Going small is a simple approach to extraordinary results, and it works. It works all the time, anywhere and on anything. Why? Because it has only one purpose—to ultimately get you to the point.

Most people who talk about SEO overcomplicate it. And for good reason. There is real potential for things to feel overcomplicated. Since so much of SEO is shrouded in a veil of secrecy, it makes sense why marketers try to make it seem so much harder than it is.

That's why Keller's quote is so suitable here. When you can focus on one thing and only one thing to succeed in SEO, the pathway forward is clear. Focus on trust. Get Google to trust you and the sky is virtually the limit. Start worrying about everything else and watch as you falter and fail.

Rather than make endless to-do lists, the focus must be

far simpler than that. It has to be laser guided. And once you understand that, the mission at hand becomes surprisingly clear. You simply have to do everything in your power to build trust. Not to compromise it or put it in jeopardy.

Part of that trust equation is to create content that's simple and understandable. To make whatever you create engaging and to the point. Don't overcomplicate things. Simplify them. Add value. And really focus on solving your customers' most pressing problems.

WHERE DO YOU STAND?

Okay. I know what you're thinking. So, if the objective here is to get Google to trust me, how exactly do I do that? Plus. How do I actually figure out how much Google trusts me right now? How do we quantify or determine that level of trust?

Sure. Knowing where you stand is important. But think about this for a moment. In any relationship, how quickly do you trust another person? It takes time, right? Especially if you've been burned in the past. So, what makes you think it's any different with Google?

Most people think that they can literally start from zero and dominate Google's search results in a matter of weeks or even months. Sure, you can make strides in that time. But there's almost no chance that Google is going to implicitly trust you enough *that quickly*.

For example, if you're in a relationship right now, how

long did it take before you really got to know and trust your spouse or significant other? Did it happen quickly? How long did it take? The answer to that question is oftentimes, years.

Now, I know. I know. We don't have years to wait around to rank our websites. But for some of the most competitive search terms, that's exactly what it takes. Years. However, this is only true if Google doesn't already trust you. If Google trusts you, ranking can happen in a matter of weeks, days and even hours.

A couple of years back, I wrote an article in Forbes, a website that Google implicitly trusts because it's been around for a very long time and so many other people that Google trusts have linked to it organically over the years. But this article was going for the motherload. Targeting a massive keyword.

I wanted to rank number one for "make money online." Now, if you know anything about online marketing, you know that this is one of the most competitive keywords on the planet. So I set out towards the challenge with the singular end in mind to rank number one.

And I did. I wrote an article titled, *21 Legit Ways To Make Money Online*. It was what you call a listicle. An article structured around creating a list of items. Google seems to love this approach (more on this later). Lists get shared often and break the article down into bite-sized chunks that are easily digestible.

It took roughly 60 days for that post to hit the illustrious number one spot. And it stayed there for well over a year, generating 2,395,532 views within the first few months. How? Google already trusts Forbes implicitly. If you build great content on a very trusted domain, it's a catalyst for exponential results.

So I wanted to test my theory on just how well it worked across the board. The following year, I attempted to rank for the same keyword. This time on Entrepreneur Magazine. And it worked. In fact, that post, titled, *7 Realistic Ways To Make Money Online*, achieved number one in record speed.

It took roughly 42 days to hit number one on Google. Now, you're probably sitting there thinking, so what? Who cares? I don't have access to a media domain where I can write content. However, here's the thing. Everyone has access to authority sites where you can create content like this.

Okay, so it's not a Forbes or Entrepreneur Magazine. But sites like YouTube, Medium.com, Quora and others are even more trusted than those domains. And everyone on the planet has access to them. Literally. Overall, there's a greater point here.

When Google trusts you implicitly, ranking is far easier. Especially, when you understand precisely how to structure your content. And I'll show you exactly how to do this. It's the same strategy I use to this day, every single time, when I build content on my blog or anywhere else.

So, since trust is so important, your job is to figure out how much Google already trusts you. Whether you're doing SEO for yourself or for a client, understanding where you stand is the key to going forward. Figuring out where you stand is the first step to achieving any goal.

Once you know just how much Google trusts you, then your singular focus should be to build that trust. Don't worry, I'll teach you how. But quantitatively, there's a lot involved. This isn't a simple task by any means. But when you understand how it works, the lightbulbs will go off.

But keep in mind that it won't be easy. Nothing worthwhile ever is. Am I right? It takes hard work. Determination. And focus. In the end, it does pay off. When your content ranks number one for a highly relevant keyword, it's like a proverbial cash machine.

Keep in mind that paid ads are great. Yet, when you rank at the top of a search result for what we call a transactional keyword (a search with the intent to purchase behind it), it's like an endless stream of customers left and right. Clearly, you understand what's at stake. Everyone does.

So if you want to figure out where you stand right now when it comes to how much Google trusts you, all you need to do is use one tool. It's called SEMRush.com. It helps you analyze the domain that you're dealing with to see what Google knows about it.

If it's brand new, then there is no trust. So you don't even have to worry about doing anything. You're starting from scratch. The drawing board, if you will. It's a tough climb for a brand-new domain name. Very tough. If that's where you're starting, then you have a long road ahead.

Remember, that's like having zero trust at all. It's like walking into a room where everyone knows each other and you're the only stranger. No one knows you. No one trusts you. You wandered into this room hoping to drum up some business, but everyone is already chatting amongst themselves.

That's what it's like when you're starting from scratch with a brand-new domain. No one knows you. No one trusts you. So ranking for any keyword is going to be a monumental task. Instead, there are other pathways forward.

Keep in mind that if you have a brand-new domain, you

can always go out there and buy an existing domain on a website like Flippa.com. An existing domain name (with content intact) that's been around for a couple of years or longer, and already has some trust, is your best bet.

Rather than starting from zero, this is a better approach. We'll dive more into this later. Clearly, you have to do your due diligence. You have to ensure that this domain name is trusted and hasn't experienced severe drop-offs on Google's SERPs (an indicator of trust violations). But it's the best path forward and can potentially save you years of effort and heartache.

SECRET 3
HOW TO RANK FASTER

I need more time, I quipped.

You don't have more time, she replied abruptly.

I hung up the phone and realized she was right. I was out of time. Out of luck. And out of money.

No one was coming to save me. It was the end of the line. The last stop. The final destination. At least, that's what I told myself. It hurt being stuck – not knowing what to do next. But that's exactly the position I found myself in.

After spending years building a business, it's hard to see it washed away. Shuttering the virtual doors and closing down the domain felt like a nail in my coffin. How could it be over like that? How did I let it get that bad?

Thinking back to that situation many years ago, I replay those events over and over in my mind. If I only had more time. That's what I kept telling myself. But I didn't have more time. Scrambling to drive organic traffic at the last minute is a tough pill to swallow.

I knew it'd be a climb. It'd be a tough battle. I was ready for that. But I was also full of excuses at first. I went in kicking and screaming. Still, I knew there was no other way to save my business.

That was when I truly appreciated the importance of time. Something I'd always taken for granted suddenly took center stage in my life. I realized time was the most precious resource I had. Not money.

Sure, money could be saved and earned, spent and thrown away. However, you could always make your money back once you lost it. But not your time. Once it's used up, it's gone for good.

I needed to compress time and learn fast. But because I was too stubborn to ask for help, I went on this journey of learning SEO alone. That was the fatal mistake. There was just too much information to absorb with too little time to make it viable.

I don't want you to make that same mistake. I want you to understand the fundamentals of SEO in an intimate way. To have the knowledge and wherewithal to make the right choices at the right time is crucial.

So what is SEO at the end of the day? Is it about keywords? Content? Link building? Up until this point, we haven't done a deep dive into the intricacies of how it all works. We've only just glossed the surface.

You see, all of these things do matter to some degree. Yes, great content is critical. Sure, you have to build links. And, obviously, the keywords that you use matter. But not as much as they used to.

Once upon a time, keywords mattered a lot. They were one of the most important aspects of ranking your content on Google's SERPs. Today, their importance has declined in the overall relevancy picture.

Now it's all about semantics. Semantics is described as the logic connected to the overall meaning of something. Google wants to understand what you mean when you search for something, which oftentimes goes beyond the literal words used.

This distinction is important when it comes to search because, long ago, it was all about the keywords and their precise order. Today, with the introduction of Hummingbird, RankBrain, and BERT, which are Google's fully overhauled semantics and natural-language engines, search is more about meaning.

Semantics is applicable to both sides of the coin. It applies to the user's search request along with the results as well. Equally important is the intention of the search. Search intent is something that Google analyzes as well.

What do I mean? For example, sometimes when you search on Google, you're merely looking for information. That means you have an informational intent. Other times, you're looking to buy something. That's transactional intent. Still, other times, you just want to go to a specific site, which is navigational intent.

The last one is when you search to compare two things. Often, there is transactional intention, but it's premature in nature. This comparison intent is meant to help you understand the difference between, say, competing products, concepts or principles.

It's important to understand that comparison intent can lead to a purchase, but it's usually looking for information related to a future purchase. Understanding the meaning of this posed difficult for Google pre-2013. Today it can do it like a pro.

Let's look at a few examples of these search intentions to better understand where keywords come into the mix here and just how Google analyzes the keywords to spit out the proper results. This information is useful to anyone looking to rank on Google's SERPs.

INFORMATIONAL SEARCH INTENT

Information is power. That much is true. And the beauty of the internet is that it has given us all the world's information at the palm of our hands. Literally. For the most part, when we search for something, we're seeking information. Plain and simple.

That information comes in many forms. We might seek information about a person, place or an event. We might ask questions like:

- Who is the president of the United States?

- LAX flight arrival delays

- How long does it take to charge a Tesla?

- Basketball scores

- How does blockchain work?

- What are the best habits to have?

- How do you make money from home?

You get the picture, right? You're searching for information on some topic. Simple enough. There are literally millions of these types of searches being performed every single second. And the results for these searches are often a combination of textual results and video results from YouTube.

Sometimes, Google will actually provide the answer itself. This is especially true when it comes to a simple question like, Who is the CEO of Google? When you ask a question like that, Google will actually give you their answer at the top.

This is also called the Google Answer Box. This is an illustrious spot to be in because it's displayed at the top of search results, highlighted inside of a box. Not all searches have this. Some do. But appearing in the Google Answer Box is certainly something to be proud of.

Google / CEO

Sundar Pichai

Oct 2, 2015–

Pichai Sundararajan, also known as Sundar Pichai, is an Indian American business executive, the chief executive officer of Alphabet Inc. and its subsidiary Google LLC. Pichai began his career as a materials engineer and joined Google as a management executive in 2004. Wikipedia

People also search for

View 15+ more

Anjali Pichai	Larry Page	Satya	Sergey Brin	Kamala	Eric	Indra Nooyi
Spouse		Nadella		Harris	Schmidt	
				Trending		

More about Sundar Pichai

Feedback

Here's one for *What are the best habits to have?* In this one, there are two featured snippets in the Google Answer Box. One is from my website, WanderlustWorker.com. The other is from DanSilvestre.com.

Google   what are the best habits to have

Q All   Shopping   Images   News   Videos   More   Settings   Tools

About 286,000,000 results (0.62 seconds)

- #1 — Best Health Habit: 10,000 Steps. ...
- #2 — Financial Habit: Expense Journaling. ...
- #3 — Success Habit: Active Goal Setting. ...
- #4 — Career Habit: Time Management. ...
- #5 — Wellness Habit: Daily Gratitude. ...
- #6 — Relationship Habit: Mindfulness. ...
- #7 — Productivity Habit: 80/20 Rule.

www.wanderlustworker.com › An Inspired Life ▾
The 7 Best Habits to Have in Life - Wanderlust Worker

**From all the habits that I've developed in my life, these are the 7 that I
consider the good daily habits that you should acquire.**

- #1 Develop a Night-Time Routine. We live in the era of busyness. ...
- #2 Exercise Regularly. ...
- #3 Eat Healthy. ...
- #4 Meditate. ...
- #6 Develop a Growth Mindset. ...
- #7 Journaling.

Feb 27, 2018

dansilvestre.com › good-daily-habits ▾
7 Good Daily Habits: How to Create an Epic Life - Dan Silvestre

About Featured Snippets   Feedback

48

TRANSACTIONAL SEARCH INTENT

Transactional search intention is the Holy Grail of search. Why? Because it has buyer intention interlaced within it. When you want to buy something, you have transactional intention. And, oftentimes, the longer the keyword used, the more transactional intention you have.

Here are a few examples of transactional intention keywords. We might start by searching for things like:

- Buy Bose headphones

- Stamps.com coupon code

- Cheap car rentals JFK

- Used MacBook Pro near me

- Costco membership price

Let's say you're in the market to buy a car. Where would

you start? Maybe with an informational intention search. You might be curious about electric cars like Teslas. And you might ask, *How long does it take to charge a Tesla?*

Notice that we didn't ask how long it takes to charge a Tesla Model X or a Tesla Model 3. We were more generic. We were simply looking for information. As the transactional search gets longer and more specific, the intention to buy increases.

Let's say we ask, *How much does a Tesla Model X Long-Range Performance cost?* That's far more specific than just asking how much it costs to buy a Tesla in general. And it means that I'm in the market for a Tesla Model X Long-Range Performance model. That's pretty specific when it comes to the details of the vehicle itself.

This is also what we call a long-tail keyword. These keywords are longer phrases that range from 4 or 5 words to even longer phrases and sentences. Today, with the introduction of natural-language processing, thanks to updates like BERT and its predecessor, Hummingbird, Google is better able to understand these queries.

Transactional intention search terms are lucrative, to say the least. And, keep in mind that the longer the long-tail keyword is, the further along people are in the buying cycle. That means, longer-tail keywords indicate that a consumer is more ready to buy than shorter ones.

It's like the difference between searching "best sneakers for men" and "best nike sneakers for men under $80 near me". The latter keyword indicates that the consumer is far more ready to purchase than the former keyword. This is an important point to keep in mind.

Since the goal of being in business is to make money, targeting these long-tail transactional keywords is key to success. Plus, the beauty of this is that it's easier to rank for long-tail keywords than short-tail keywords. And for good reason. Short-tail keywords have more informational intent.

It's like the difference between searching "houses with pools" and "houses in Phoenix with pools less than $500,000". Can you see how the former has more informational intent and the latter has transactional intention? A person searching the latter is further along in the buying cycle.

This is potentially important to a real estate agent in Phoenix who might be targeting people looking for homes less than $500k with pools. So, they might go about creating content targeting those types of searches. Do you see how this matters in the grand scheme of things?

My goal isn't just to educate you on ranking high on search, but also to help give you a laser-guided approach to actually turning your search results into traffic, leads, and ultimately, sales. Once you understand the mechanics of all this, you'll come to see that there is a very specific formula for success.

NAVIGATIONAL SEARCH INTENT

Navigational search intention simply means that you're looking to navigate to a particular place on the internet. You could be looking to login to your Facebook account, or find a particular guide by some website, amongst other things.

If you're curious about some examples of what a navigational search actually looks like, here's several:

- Facebook login

- SEMRush account login

- LADWP payment history

- NameCheap domain dashboard

- MOZ SEO Guide

COMPARISON SEARCH INTENT

Comparison search intention is exactly what it sounds look. It's when you're looking to compare and contrast things. Sometimes it is transactional in nature, but not exactly. For example, you could be looking for the best doctors in your area, but not have transactional intent just yet.

Often, these searches start with the word "best" or "top", for example. Other words like "cheapest" or "affordable" are often more related to transactional intent. This is one of those areas that are murkier. Here are a few examples:

- Best family-friendly SUVs

- What are the best habits to have?

- Top remote jobs

ROBERT KANAAT

- Safest sedans to drive

- Best daycares near me

RESEARCHING KEYWORDS

So here's the question that most people ask. How do you find the right keywords to rank for? Is it just a matter of going after the most popular, highly competitive phrases? The truth is that the answer depends on just how much Google trusts you.

If you're just starting out with a brand-new domain, you have just about zero pre-built trust with Google. So, you have to ask yourself, where are you starting? The goal at the outset is to target keywords that are not as competitive. That means going after long-tail transactional keywords with less demand.

If you have no trust built with Google, you'll find it an uphill battle to go after high-competition keywords. That's why where you start is paramount to the strategy you put into place. Targeting less competitive keywords is always a win-win, whether you're just starting out or you've built up a bit of trust in the past.

For example, let's say that you own a used car dealership in Orlando, Florida. The ideal keyword (and most obvious one) would be "used cars Orlando". But how hard do you think it'll be to rank for that kind of keyword, especially with a brand-new domain? It will be very challenging to say the least.

However, if you have years of domain history and a site with great content geared towards helping consumers buy used cars, that's a different story. It all depends on where you're starting. Newcomers would target different long-tail keywords that were transactional in nature than a short-tail keyword.

When you sit down to brainstorm, keep in mind that highly competitive keywords, although attractive, should be avoided at the outset. The goal for brainstorming is really to research an array of ideas that can be used to target users interested in your product, service or niche who are further along in the buying cycle.

When we talk about research, we're actually referring to the hard numbers. What does that mean? It means making data-driven decisions. We want to find out:

- Approximately how many monthly searches are being performed for that particular keyword.

- Is the keyword a long-tail keyword?

- What is the search intention behind the chosen phrase?

- How much competition currently exists, and will it be possible to rank on the first page in a reasonable amount of time?

Now, the tool used for doing this is called the Keyword Planner Tool and it comes from the search giant itself. But the Keyword Planner Tool is really a tool that is meant for advertisers that are looking to place ads on Google's network, so it has its limitations.

However, even though it's a tool for advertisers, it does offer some of the best insights into searches being conducted on Google in real-time. Specifically, the important insights lay within the competition and search volumes of those keywords.

When you conduct a search using the Keyword Planner Tool, Google presents you with a variety of results along with the level of competition and the number of global monthly searches. It can also present you with a number of similar search results.

However, the competition you're seeing (low, medium or high) does not equate to how hard it is to rank for that keyword. It only relates to how competitive it is to have your ad rank for that keyword. So, you need to use another tool to determine that, which we'll look at shortly.

So let's see just how this works. Point your browser to adwords.google.com/KeywordPlanner or simply Google "Keyword Planner Tool" and click on the first result. When you get to the screen, it will ask you to sign into your Adwords account.

If you don't have an Adwords account, you can set one up. It won't cost you anything. But you will need a Google account to get this going. When you get to the Keyword Planner page, you'll have two initial options on what to do next:

1. Discover new keywords

2. Get search volumes and forecasts

If you've done your research and created a list of long-tail keywords, you would select the second option on the list "Get search volume and forecasts." This will allow us to just copy and paste your brainstorming keywords into Keyword Planner (or upload a CSV file).

But you can also select the first option if you want to merely discover new keywords. For example, if you want to search for new keywords, you could find out what Google has in mind or would suggest to you based on products or services related to your business.

For example, starting with "used cars Orlando" and turning off the branded search results, you get the following keywords:

- Buy here pay here Orlando

- Cars for sale Orlando

- Orlando auto mall

- Buy here pay here Orlando FL

- Orlando car dealerships

- Buy here pay here Orlando 500 down

- Used cars for sale Orlando

- Used cars Orlando under 5000

- Used cars Orlando under 2000

Can you see how this might be helpful in creating long-tail transactional keywords? You can actually spot some of the long-tail keywords in this list. And you can see just how many search results it produces. If you've never placed ads on Google Adwords, the average monthly searches will display as a range like "100 – 1K" or "1K – 10K". Otherwise, you'll see more precise figures.

You can also put in the domain name of your competitor and get search results based on that. For example, we could use the domain orlandopreowned.com to help find suggestions. This means we would use the second option stating, "start with a website."

When we start with a website to discover new keywords, we get the following examples from a very long list:

- Orlando preowned

- Orlando preowned cars

- Orlando pre owned cars

- Orlando pre owned Orlando FL

- Pre owned cars in Orlando FL

- Pre owned cars Orlando FL

- Orlando FL used car dealership

- Used car lots in Orlando Florida

Now, when we look at the meta description tag of this website (by viewing the source code on the home page), we see the following description: *Orlando Preowned is a dealership located near Orlando Florida. We're here to help with any automotive needs you may have. Don't forget to check out our used cars.*

This description is no longer as relevant as it once was. However, it does help to solidify what the page is about. Gone are the meta keywords that once used to be important. They are no longer used at all. Today, Google gathers the keywords based on the content and links pointing to the site and on the site itself.

Keep that in mind when you're doing your research and your due diligence. But also remember that your chances for ranking for keywords like this are based on your historical level of trust with Google. When we analyze this site with the Wayback Machine, we see that it was purchased by this dealership in early 2018.

SEMRush also indicates that there are a few hundred backlinks to the site as well, indicating that they've been hard at work building the organic link profile of the site. We'll get more into the mechanics of this later. For now, just understand that it meets the threshold of historical trust.

KEYWORD DISCOVERY

If you haven't already done your brainstorming for keywords, now's the time to do it. As you can see, there are numerous ways to discover keywords. You can do this using the Google Keyword Planner, along with other methods.

For now, let's focus on getting search volume and forecasts based on a list of keywords. Here, you'll find a box for entering those keywords. You can enter them in one line at a time, or by using commas to separate each keyword. Again, you could also upload a CSV file of a list of keywords if you're so inclined.

When you use the other option to discover keywords, you can also select things like the language and the location. These are pre-filled in for you, but you could modify those selections. For example, the default is targeting the United States and that's based on my location. But you could target only a specific location, if you're offering a local service, somewhere else for example, and you don't want to target everyone in the country.

Keep in mind that this tool is meant for advertisers on Google's Adwords platform. It's not meant as a way to get the search volume and competition for every single keyword. This is the drawback behind the system. In the past, it was far easier to see search volumes and competition, but all that has now changed.

You can, of course, shorten your keywords to estimate traffic for short-tail keywords, but that won't help you in your approach to SEO. Your focus should remain on long-tail transactional keywords. Focus on phrases and sentences that you think would be popular questions in your field.

But, let's say for a moment that we don't get any results when we paste in our long-tail keywords. What else can we do? Well, we can continue brainstorming to come up with new ideas, or even start to type keywords into Google's search bar so that we can see them from its autosuggestion tool.

You've undoubtedly used the autosuggestion many times in the past. When you begin to type in "best dress shoes" for example, and hit the space bar, you're presented with a number of the top suggestions for searches that are being performed on Google for this particular term.

Unfortunately, these are not ordered by the most searched down to the least searched. No, Google keeps us guessing with that. But we could type these terms into the Keyword Planner Tool to complete our research. So, as you can see from the following list, here's what we get when we type in "best dress shoes" then add a space to see what Google suggests.

```
Q  best dress shoes

Q  best dress shoes - Google Search
Q  best dress shoes for men
Q  best dress shoes for plantar fasciitis
Q  best dress shoes for flat feet
Q  best dress shoes under 200
Q  best dress shoes for walking
```

1. Best dress shoes (short-tail keyword)

2. Best dress shoes for men (long-tail keyword)

3. Best dress shoes for plantar fasciitis (long-tail keyword)

4. Best dress shoes for flat feet (long-tail keyword)

5. Best dress shoes under 200 (long-tail keyword)

6. Best dress shoes for walking (long-tail keyword)

As you can see by the list that we generated using Google's autosuggestion tool, there are plenty of options for writing great content. Additionally, it might present you with ideas that you might not have considered earlier during your brainstorming session.

For example, number three on the list talks about "Plantar Fasciitis," or "Jogger's Heel," a condition that develops as a result of usually over-exercising, from weight, or age.

We certainly see an idea here for creating content that contains massive value by not only breaking down this ailment, but also in analyzing shoes from this perspective. Which dress shoes for men are the best for those afflicted with jogger's heel?

The fourth result talks about flat feet. That's another great idea for a post. What are the best dress shoes for men who have flat feet? These long-tail keywords are excellent for ranking quickly on Google's SERPs. But the content has to be great, so always keep that in mind.

Now, we can also expand our search into other types of shoes to see what kind of results we come up with. Remember, autosuggestion is a great tool to use if your original list brings back no results. So, here are a few examples of different types of shoes for men.

1. Best dress shoes for men

2. Best winter shoes for men

3. Best hiking boots for men

4. Best formal shoes for men

5. Best beach sandals for men

When we conduct our search using the long-tail keywords through the Keyword Planner, our results indicate the number of monthly searches being performed, plus the level of competition.

For the search results, we can see that through the Keyword Planner that "Best dress shoes for men," is a relatively popular search with around 1,900 searches per month and high competition. This was reinforced by Google's autosuggestion.

Again, the competition level applies to advertisers that are looking to buy ads for this keyword. Still, it does give you a sense of the search volume and how competitive searches are for this long-tail keyword search.

Although high competition here doesn't necessarily equate to high competition in organic search results, the two usually end up being relatively similar.

The understanding here is that advertisers that are looking to compete heavily on certain keyword searches through Google's AdWords, are doing so because the organic search is also very competitive and hard to rank for. For this reason, advertisers are also going after paid search.

Keyword (by relevance)		Avg. monthly searches ?	Competition ?	Suggested... ?	Ad impr. s... ?	Add to plan
Best dress shoes for men	⤴	1,900	High	$0.96	–	✓
Best hiking boots for men	⤴	1,600	High	$0.80	–	»
Best winter shoes for men	⤴	210	High	$1.26	–	»
Best formal shoes for men	⤴	140	High	$0.30	–	»
Best beach sandals for men	⤴	30	High	$0.58	–	»

However, this still hinders our ability to truly have x-ray vision into Google's results. How are we supposed to work on optimizing keywords and searches for long-tail keywords when we don't know precisely how competitive organic searches are as opposed to paid searches?

Unfortunately, Google doesn't provide a tool for allowing us to peer into the inner workings of their organic search. That's the core reason why Google is, well, Google. Some things simply can't be revealed to the public for fear of abuse to the system.

Google already went through a major ordeal to clean up its SERPs many years ago due to Black-Hat SEOs and thin-content sites that were primarily seeking to rank by utilizing virtually any means that were available to them.

For that reason, and many other reasons, Google just doesn't want to reveal too much. However, we can use other tools to glean some more information from Google's SERPs. Although, in a perfect world, Google would be more transparent, there are some next-best solutions.

One of those next-best solutions is the SEO Quake Plugin tool. I've spoken about this tool before in the past and I believe in it a great deal. It's an excellent resource for determining your chances of ranking for a particular keyword search by displaying some important information.

The information that SEO Quake reveals allows us to get a better sense of a Webpage's authority and age, two of the core components in Google's pyramid of trust.

SEO QUAKE PLUGIN

The SEO Quake Plugin helps people peer into Google's search results to see what's going on behind the scenes. This is helpful from a trust perspective because it displays just how Google sees the listings on its SERPs.

We can leverage this information by conducting searches on Google for our long-tail keywords, then analyzing the search results. I'll show you how to determine the difficulty for ranking for a particular search using this exact method.

So how does this work?

Well, the first step is to download and install the SEO Quake Plugin tool. However, one quick suggestion – I don't recommend doing this on your primary browser. For example, if you use Chrome as your primary browser, download and install this on Firefox. If you use Firefox, do it on Chrome, and so on.

Ensuring that you don't use this on your primary browser is important. SEO Quake adds extraneous data into every search that you conduct on Google, and sometimes slows your searches down. It's great for the purpose of keyword research, but not so great for everyday usage.

Now, let's head back and conduct those long-tail keyword searches while using the SEO Quake Plugin tool. But, what information, particularly, is this tool going to give us? Well, it's going to show us just how trusted Google deems a particular listing.

Also, a note before you start – you can turn on and off different settings for the SEO Quake Plugin tool from the preferences menu for the extension in the browser. After using the tool on a few searches, you might come to find certain factors more important than others.

When we conduct a search for the first one of our long-tail keywords, namely – "Best dress shoes for men" – we get a set of results that displays standard SERP listings. In the result set, we can see the listings, but also under each listing, we see a bar with some statistics and data.

We can see the R, or Rank of a page, its Alexa Ranking, its Bing ranking, the number of links to the domain, number of links for that page, the historical age of the domain, and also a link to the website source data to analyze the underlying codebase.

The top three listings, which are displayed in the proceeding image, can give you an indication of the difficulty to rank for this long-tail keyword. One important thing to note here is that Google will type out the words used in the description to fetch its results in bold format.

So, when we're looking at the top result, for example, we can see that the title is "10 Best Men's Dress Shoes Every Man Should Own - The …" The description has bold lettering for the words "best men's dress shoes." It's clear that Google is using these main words to fetch these results.

If you take a closer look at the first listing, you'll see that it has an Alexa ranking of 16.2K, symbolized by the "a" icon. The Alexa ranking is a categorization of all of the Websites on the Internet into chronological order. With Alexa, number 1 is the most popular site in the world, and the numbering goes up from there.

What you'll also see here is that the second listing has an Alexa ranking of 2.78K, which is higher than the ranking of the first listing at 16.2K, yet it remains in the second position. You can also see that it has 159 links (L) to the actual page whereas the first result has 289 links to the page.

The second listing, which is for esquire.com, also has more links to the actual domain name itself. Esquire.com has 12.4 million links to the domain whereas thetrendspotter.net has a paltry 2 million links. Yet, thetrendspotter.net is outperforming esquire.com on this search.

Thus, the "L" and the "LD" for links to the page and links to the domain represent two very important pieces of information, respectively. The reason listing number 1 is appearing before 2, even though its overall domain is ranked lower, has to do with the page-level factors that are involved.

Why?

As we can see, listing number two has more links to its domain. But, what still remains to be seen is why listing number one is ranking ahead of listing number two? Plus, we can see that Esquire.com is an older domain. It dates back to 2000 as opposed to 2012 for thetrendspotter.net.

However, you also have to keep in mind that the age of the actual page and how many backlinks it has is clearly more important in this instance. Since the content is thin on both sites, the other trust factors come into play in order to help provide the deciding factor.

One piece of information that you can't garner from these listings is just how good the content is that's written on the listings' respective pages. Unless of course you go read each listing's content, which might pose as useful to you, you'll be unable to determine how good they are.

The competition for this search is fierce because as you move down the list, you'll see that each of the SERP listings have a huge number of links going to their domains, making them incredibly popular. Unless you dish out an extraordinary piece of content on an authority site, ranking for this search will be hard.

So, what are you supposed to do?

Well, your next task is to try conducting your SEO Quake research using the autosuggestions as well. What do the top results look like for those searches? What are your chances of ranking high for one of Google's autosuggestions that you uncovered?

This isn't an exact science by any means, but it is a way to make an educated guess on where to spend your time. Keep in mind that the content writing is going to be an exhaustive endeavor for you, so be sure that your limited resource of time is focused in the right direction.

SECRET 4
CREATING AUTHORITY

Growing up, one of my all-time favorite actors to watch was Tom Cruise. Ever since I saw *Risky Business*, he became a legend in my eyes. Maybe it was because I really enjoyed the film itself. His acting was incredibly authentic and believable.

That film was a coming-of-age comedy of a high school student's extraordinary adventure that occurs when his wealthy parents go out of town. If you've seen the flick, you know the plot. I know it's an older movie, but Cruise's acting led to it being his break-out role. And for good reason.

Risky Business was a great film. But here's the thing that happens. Once you relate to a character's role, you begin to follow that character. I still remember when *Top Gun* first came out. I literally clamored to see that film. Even though I was too young at the time to see it in the theaters, I managed to catch it once it came to television.

After *Top Gun*, it was movies like *Cocktail, Rain Man* and *Days of Thunder* that helped continue Cruise's iconic roles, and solidified him as a superstar, A-List actor. Today, I still catch all the *Mission Impossible* films. They're the perfect mixture of drama with action-packed, teeth-gritting suspense.

So why do I tell you this? For a very specific purpose. We all have actors, musicians and other celebrities who we like and follow. And for good reason. We've consumed some piece of their content (or multiple pieces) that we've connected with. And for that reason, they have authority in our eyes.

Movie studios know how important this is. They know that if they pay big money to a famed celebrity to star in their film, that they'll have an instant, pre-built audience ready to go. Why? Because big-named actors and actresses carry huge levels of authority. Tom Cruise brings massive authority to a movie.

Simply his name itself can generate tens of millions, to hundreds of millions of dollars for any film, production company or distribution partner. In films, music and other mediums, authority is massive. Think about the film, *Ocean's 11*. That film starred so many well-known actors that it's dizzying.

But they knew very well that people would come just for those names. And indeed, they did. That film has spawned many, many offshoots like *Ocean's 12, Ocean's 13* and more. I say this because of how important this concept of authority is. Both in the real world and the digital world.

For example, I receive hundreds of requests every single month for guest posts and links on my blog wanderlustworker.com. Why do you think that is? It's because that domain carries authority. And the ability to publish content on the domain holds a certain level of importance to it.

That's because authority is one of the core concepts and principles of SEO. What is authority? How is it built? And who gets to define what authority really means? Well, let's think about the word itself first. What does it mean to have authority and who can actually command it?

If we think about the business world, someone like the president or chief executive officer of a company wields authority. They're in a position of power because they worked to get to that level. They either started the business or worked their way up over time.

The same concept applies in the entertainment world. Who has commanding authority there? Well, producers and directors for one, but also well-known actors like Tom Cruise. How did they get there? Through hard work and dedication. It didn't happen overnight.

We also see this concept in sports. Sports stars have authority in their given professions. From basketball to football, to soccer, baseball, and hockey, no matter what sport we talk about, the players are the authorities there. They've built up their skills over years and years of practice and hard work, along with a cult-like following.

So, authority is something that's built up over time, right? Well, yes, exactly. And that means that if your Website is brand new, you're going to be lacking authority. So why is this important? Well, Google won't trust you if you lack authority.

Think about it this way. How likely are you to see a film with no big-name actors in it? Films are released all the time. And often, we rush to see films with our favorite actors or actresses in them first. We brush aside films with newcomers and no-name actors. Even though they might be great films, unless they win an award, their audience is limited.

In fact, this concept of authority is heavily steeped in trust. We trust big-name actors and brand-name companies alike because of our experiences with them. There's a history there. Past exchanges. And because of that past experience, they've built authority in our eyes over time.

For some people, it's all about authority. Let's say you go shopping in the supermarket for instance. Some will only buy products from authority brands they trust like Colgate or Gillette, for example. They won't buy the generic, store brands. Not everyone of course. But brands have built up businesses based on a history of trust-based, authoritative exchanges.

It's no different in the banking world, as well. Let's say, for example, that a new business goes to the bank for a loan. The bank officer asks for some business credentials such as past years' tax returns or income statements. But there are none to produce because it's a new business.

How likely is that new business to get a loan? Not likely at all, unless of course there's a personal guarantee from a director, principle, or officer. In that case, sure, the bank would likely extend a loan depending on the creditworthiness of the individual making the personal guarantee.

However, in the SEO world, it doesn't work quite as simply as that. Authority is something that's built up over time, and not something that happens overnight. This is also why Websites that have been around for a long time (i.e. 5 years or longer) always rank higher on Google's SERPs.

Websites that have been around for a long time and have steadily built up authority by creating meaningful content and getting meaningful links from other trusted sites on the Web, will always appear higher up on the SERPs.

In a way, Google created this all-important limiting factor for a particular reason. It's not easy to climb up the SERPs any longer without authority. And it's impossible to build authority unless it's done over time. So, authority is something that's earned, not overnight, but steadily over years.

So, where does that leave us? How are we supposed to do SEO when we lack authority? Well, that topic certainly warrants a discussion. But to summarize for now, authority is going to be built by leveraging existing sites that Google already trusts. To do this, you simply create high-value content on trusted sites with links back to your own unique high-value content.

Sound like a lot of work? Well it is! No one said that SEO was going to be easy. Be prepared to dig your heels in and grind away.

HOW TO CREATE AUTHORITY

There's a huge misconception in the digital world.

Way back when Google first started, they set about on a mission. Their mission was simple. It was to organize the world's information. To enact this mission, they created a simple algorithm that would spider the web to rank content relevantly.

Their first core algorithm was called PageRank. Today, it's mostly meaningless, even though Google does claim it's still a ranking signal. But to truly understand the mechanics of authority, you have to understand how this formula works.

$$PageRank \ of \ site = \sum \frac{PageRank \ of \ inbound \ link}{Number \ of \ links \ on \ that \ page}$$

OR

$$PR(u) = (1 - d) + d \times \sum \frac{PR(v)}{N(v)}$$

In the digital world, authority is created by getting other people that Google already trusts to link to you. This old PageRank formula essentially says that the rank of a page is equal to the sum of the quality of its inbound links.

This was originally derived from the PageRank of the inbound link divided by the total number of links. So, if a page has a PageRank of 3 and there are 10 outbound links on it, the PageRank passed over is 0.3. Take all the links into a page from all sources and you would get the PageRank.

While the mathematics aren't as important, here's the primary concept to understand. PageRank is created by the quality of the inbound links to a page. It's much more important to get links from sites that have a high PageRank rather than a low one.

Today, link building is still a central part of SEO. And it's the way that authority is created. While the formulas have morphed and transformed to other more recent ones, this central theme still holds true. That's why it's important to understand it.

The formula for PageRank generates a number derived by analyzing the quantity and quality of the links directed to any page. In the previous example we analyzed with the SEO Quake tool, we looked at the search "best dress shoes for men."

In that search, we noticed that esquire.com, a website with massive amounts of authority, was outranked by a newer site called thetrendspotter.net. If you'll recall, however, esquire.com only had 159 links to its content on the topic, whereas thetrendspotter.net had 289 links.

And this is where things get interesting. Because, Google is using the PageRank formula (amongst other computations) to determine that the content produced by thetrendspotter.net is more valuable than esquire.com. This is largely because of the link profile to that particular page.

Notice, this is not about the link profile to the entire domain. Esquire.com crushes thetrendspotter.net with over 10 million more links to its domain. But that doesn't help it here. Google has determined that thetrendspotter.net has a more relevant piece of content, partially due to its PageRank.

Now, understand this. It's not about the quantity of links. It's about the quality and quantity of links. They must be authentic. Organic. Have diverse origins, meaning they aren't all from the same site. And the actual PageRank of the pages that are linking to it are also crucial.

Meaning, you're not wasting your time by doing shady things like buying links or generating them through bots. Nor are you trading links. Those practices will destroy your chances of ranking. No, what's happening here is the creation of authentic, meaningful links from topical sites that matter. And it's happening organically and diversely over time.

This is how Google PageRank works. So keep in mind that it's not just about creating content and letting it sit there. The organic link profile of the content has to be healthy. Meaning, relevant, topical sites need to be creating their own natural, organic and high-quality content that's linking in.

Historically, speaking, the PageRank formula produced a number between zero and ten. Zero being the lowest. Ten being the highest PageRank that a site can have. While no longer publicly used or measurable, understand that this baseline number tells Google the importance of the page itself. Not the domain.

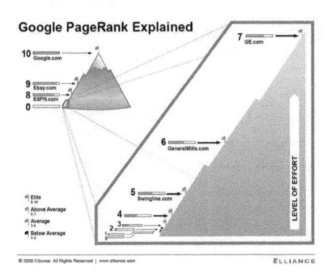

As you can see in the following image depicted here of PageRank done by Elliance, Inc. way back in 2006, it helps to indicate the level of difficulty involved with moving up this so-called mountain that we call PageRank on the Web.

Again, PageRank is a core algorithm that is no longer relevant. But the concept is incredibly relevant. And it helps to paint the picture of difficulty that stands between you and your ability to create real authority. In the image, you can see the monumental undertaking involved with going from

5 to 6, let alone from 9 to 10.

But don't let this dissuade you. There is a pathway forward. And this information just helps to give historical context to the importance of relevancy. But the key concept to take away is simply this. Link building is still a critical aspect of SEO. Without it, you won't make any real strides.

But how do you build authority? Meaning, how do you get other people that Google already trusts to link to you? It's not easy. That should be obvious by now. But there is a core strategy that offers the most effective results for the time spent.

Keep in mind that although links are central concept to creating authority, they must be authentic and organic. Do not attempt to purchase links in bulk ever. And I do mean ever. If you do, you can effectively destroy your authority before you ever create it.

Many newcomers are drawn into the illusion that buying hundreds (or thousands) of links on Fiverr, Freelancer or other platforms, will actually help them rank for a keyword. Newsflash. It won't. And the more you do this, the faster your rank will drop.

Instead, here's how you have to approach authority. The goal here is to rank your site relevantly for keywords that matter. This is done, not by trying to spam links or articles, but by creating authentic content that creates real value.

That's where your most valuable links will come from. Just think about it this way. When you see a great piece of content, aren't you compelled to tell others about it? Sure, you are. You share it on social media, and link to it in chat. You might even blog about it.

The nature of authority is created like this. You build great content that people naturally want to link to. It's natural, organic and the safest way you can build authority. And simply put, it doesn't happen overnight. It will take time.

Of course, there is a process for doing this. Here are the steps involved:

1. Create valuable anchor content that helps solve problems

2. Build equally valuable content on authority websites

3. Ensure your authority site content links to your anchor content

4. Chop down content into bite-sized pieces shareable on social media

5. Engage in outreach with influencers, bloggers and media professionals

6. Rinse and repeat the process

STEP #1 – CREATE VALUABLE ANCHOR CONTENT THAT HELPS SOLVE PROBLEMS

First, let's address the obvious. In business, you make money by solving problems. Those problems could be big problems or small problems. The amount of money is always in direct proportion to the size of the problems you solve.

Once you've identified the top problems your customers are facing, you have to create valuable anchor content that helps solve those problems. Anchor content is simply content that resides on your website. On your company's domain.

Keep in mind that your best content should always live on *your* domain. Always. Take the time to create an informative piece of content that truly solves the most pressing problems your customers have. Now, you might be saying to yourself, well, I'm not a writer. So now what?

You don't have to be a world-class writer to create content that solves problems. Certainly, you can hire an expert to help you craft a great piece of content. You can also create video content or audio, and have it transcribed, then optimized by an SEO expert.

There are many options on the table. But the important thing to understand is that you have to give away the farm. Literally. You have to pull back the curtain and flood them with value. Think that's crazy? I assure you that it's not.

Keep in mind that you're competing with millions of others. If you don't go all out and give them an insane amount of value, they won't take notice. Think about it yourself. When you see a great piece of content that addresses your problem, don't you want to share it with others?

When your content is valuable, in-depth, and directly helps solve a pressing problem, people take notice. So does Google. This type of content is rare to find. But it's also the type of content found at the top of Google search results for a reason. It stands out.

No matter how you slice it, even when you craft excellent content, it takes time to rank. Even on the most popular domains, content won't rank overnight for highly competitive search terms. It will take days or weeks. On less popular domains, that time length is even longer.

So what makes content valuable? Aside from solving your customers' problems, here's what this translates into:

1. The content should be in the range of 1,800-2,200 words

2. It should be keyword-optimized for one primary keyword

3. There should be a keyword-rich title that creates curiosity

4. The URL should contain the primary keyword or a simplified variation of it

5. It should be well-written and free of spelling or grammatical errors

6. Easy to read (Flesch-Kinkaid score of 80 or higher)

7. Sources should be cited where necessary

8. The content should have at least 2 to 3 relevant external links

9. It should have at least 2 to 3 internal links to relevant content on the anchor site

10. Should use multimedia (photos and videos) to help illustrate concepts or provide walkthroughs for better understanding

Although not an exhaustive list, these 10 key points will help you craft your anchor content that ranks. Keep in mind that if you don't feel confident enough to do this yourself, you should hire a professional. Your anchor content is a vital part of your business. Treat it with the respect it deserves.

Another point to illuminate is this. If your domain name is fairly new with little to no existing content, don't expect to rank for competitive keywords right away. Google doesn't trust newcomers. Simply put. It's all about longevity and consistency here.

ROBERT KANAAT

STEP #2 – BUILD EQUALLY VALUABLE ANCHOR CONTENT ON AUTHORITY SITES

Once you've gone through the process of building your anchor content on your domain, your job isn't done. Your next task is to create equally valuable authority site content. What's an authority site? It's simply a website that anyone can publish to that's already trusted by Google.

For example, YouTube is one authority site that should be a major focus for you. Why? Because YouTube is the second largest search engine in the world. Plus, there is a major focus on video today. And, creating video content can help better illuminate written content.

Why use authority sites? Remember, they're highly trusted by Google. And, when you create valuable content on an authority site, the results are far quicker. Plus, when

88

your authority content links to your anchor content, you supercharge your results.

Of course, there are many authority sites you can choose from. The list is fairly extensive. However, your focus should be only on the primary ones that are relevant today. While there are many you could use, here's a list of the ones you should focus on:

1. YouTube

2. Medium

3. Quora

4. LinkedIn Publishing

5. Reddit

6. WordPress

7. Blogger

8. Tumblr

9. Scribd

10. Vimeo

Content Marketing

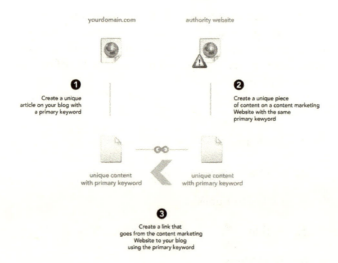

yourdomain.com   authority website

1 Create a unique article on your blog with a primary keyword

2 Create a unique piece of content on a content marketing Website with the same primary keyword

unique content with primary keyword   unique content with primary keyword

3 Create a link that goes from the content marketing Website to your blog using the primary keyword

When you create content on authority sites, you're doing something called content marketing. You're marketing your existing anchor content on authority sites. You're doing this because authority sites are highly trusted and a single link from them is very powerful.

When you create content on authority sites, it's also far more likely to rank before any content you create on your own domain. That's because the authority site has a high domain rank. But that doesn't mean it's guaranteed to rank because you'll still need links to the content you create.

Popular creators on authority sites who have large followings get substantial benefits from posting. Not only is the authority site content more likely to rank, but when that authority site content is shared by others, it creates an exponential effect.

That doesn't mean you have to be a popular creator to utilize this strategy. You don't. The point is that this method works because authority sites are already trusted by Google. And when you create content on those sites linking to your own site, it creates a very important trust bridge.

It's exactly like asking someone you already trust for a recommendation for a doctor or a dentist, or any other person, place or business for that matter. When someone you already trust refers you to someone else they trust, there's a transference of trust that occurs.

STEP #3 – ENSURE YOUR AUTHORITY SITE CONTENT LINKS TO YOUR ANCHOR CONTENT

The next step in the authority creation stage is to ensure that authority site content links back to your anchor content. However, you have to do this with tact and not overdo it. All you need is one solid link back. It should link back with the primary keyword or a variation of it.

For example, if you're optimizing for *Boston Orthodontist*, your link back from the authority site could be *Boston Dentist* or *Boston Orthodonture* and of course, *Boston Orthodontist*. All of these achieve the same results. But it could also be a generic link like *learn more* or *book an appointment.*

Your goal is to be as natural and organic as possible when linking back to your site. The point is that each piece of authority site content that you build should link back to one piece of anchor content on your site. Not to the home page of your site.

Remember, you're creating a bridge. And the more bridges to different pages you have, the better. This builds diversity in your link structure, which is important to Google. Keep in mind that they track everything right down to the velocity of links being created and the IP addresses of those links.

They use all this data to determine the organic nature of the link building. That's important to them because Google cares very much about how truly relevant a piece of content is, along with the domain that it resides at. Considering all this, you really do have to put in an honest effort when doing any sort of SEO work.

But don't overthink it. All you have to remember here is to create one link that goes from the authority site content to your anchor content. I know, it sounds easy and straightforward. Except for the fact that the content itself will take you time to create.

ROBERT KANAAT

STEP #4 – CHOP DOWN CONTENT INTO BITE-SIZED PIECES SHAREABLE ON SOCIAL MEDIA

This next step in the process is crucial, especially when first launching your content. All you need to do here is to chop it down into bite-sized pieces so that it's shareable on social media. Meaning, create a summary of your post or clips of your video. Then, share it on social media platforms.

It's important to do this early on. This will help give your content traction. People will click on it and if it's engaging and valuable enough, they'll share it. Most social media networks have algorithms that frown on link usage in the posts. To avoid that, you can post your link in the first comment.

However, if you're doing this, there are some things to note. First is to never spam your following. Ever. Create

94

engaging posts that aren't just about self-promotion, but about the topic or niche or industry you're in. This also sets you up as an authority.

Most social media algorithms also favor those who comment and interact with others. So, don't simply post your own content and avoid interacting with others. You'll need to make the *Algorithm Gods* happy if you're going to get some traction.

Another important point to note here is that you should not be doing this yourself. You should create an SOP (Standard Operating Procedure) using Trello or some other workflow tool. Find a virtual assistant on a platform like Upwork and outsource this.

Whether it's cutting down the video into a clip while overlaying subtitles, or simply summarizing a post, create a system with processes and people to execute on this. Then share and post it on social media channels like Facebook, Instagram, Twitter and others.

If you're not a social person, this will feel hard for you to do. I get it. You don't want to seem like you're selling or pitching something. You'll silently say, *but what will others think of me?* And you know what? Do it anyways. If it feels uncomfortable, lean into that discomfort because that's where growth occurs.

ROBERT KANAAT

STEP #5 – ENGAGE IN OUTREACH WITH INFLUENCERS, BLOGGERS AND MEDIA PROFESSIONALS

My friend and mentor, Russell Brunson, popularized a concept created by Chet Holmes called the Dream 100. The Dream 100 works like this. Make a list of the top 100 people in your industry who you would love to work with. They're people who already have large or substantial audiences and followers.

Here's the reasoning behind this. It's better to spend the time doing outreach and connecting with people who already have a large audience than it is to start from scratch. Although, keep in mind that this will take substantial outreach and a willingness to give value to others.

However, no matter what industry you're in, you can connect with the top bloggers, influencers and media professionals by using the Dream 100 approach. Keep in mind that some of these individuals have substantial lists with hundreds of thousands, sometimes millions, of people.

Here's how this works.

1. Make a list of your Dream 100

2. Subscribe to their podcasts, YouTube channels and email lists

3. Follow them on all social media platforms

4. Learn 2 or 3 personal things about them that you find similar (i.e. they have children the same age as yours, they grew up in a town near you, etc.)

5. Write a well-crafted series of letters introducing yourself, and creating a connection with the individual

6. Find their mailing address

7. Mail them something of value and include your letter in brightly colored, odd-shaped packaging

8. Take a photo of the package, mail it then follow up on social media

9. Rinse and repeat weekly until you connect with them

Yes, this is a process. But imagine the amount of progress you can make by just connecting with one media professional, popular blogger or influencer. What could they do for your business? This works for link building just as much as it does for guest blogging or even affiliate marketing relationships.

ROBERT KANAAT

STEP #6 – RINSE AND REPEAT THE PROCESS

This strategy is not something that will help you outrank your competition overnight. It will take time. As long as you stay consistent, it does work. You simply need to put in the time and the sweat equity by rinsing and repeating the process every week.

Weekly? Yes. You have to do this on a weekly basis. Creating content takes time. I understand that. But you need to stay consistent with this, along with your outreach. But the beauty about this is that you can create systems and processes for managing these tasks.

Trello is a vital tool that you should use when implementing this strategy. Trello is simple to use and an easy way to assign tasks to other individuals. It'll also let you track the progress of tasks through what are called boards.

I won't dive into a deep discussion about Trello, but if you don't already know how to use it, I'd highly suggest learning it. Trello has been an instrumental tool for me in the SEO field. It will help to structure and organize your workflow.

Whether you're an aspiring SEO consultant or just a business owner looking to crush your competition on search, Trello is a great way to manage all the tasks you need to do. Sign up, create a free account, and start your first few boards.

Boards are like buckets where you organize different lists. For example, I have 4 separate boards on my Trello:

- To Do

- In Progress

- For Review

- Completed

When I want to assign a task, I place it in my, *To Do* board and I can assign it to an individual. When the task is in progress, it's moved from the, *To Do* board to the, *In Progress* board. When the task is completed, it's moved to the, *For Review* board. After confirmation and a quick quality control, it's then moved to the *Completed* board.

I don't know about you, but I absolutely love workflow tools like this. You can assign deadlines, get notifications of on-going tasks from your team, and see when things might be falling through the cracks. It's vital and I would highly suggest you give it a test drive.

SECRET 5
AGE IS MORE THAN A NUMBER

How old are you, kid?

A family friend was asking. He was older, maybe in his 50's or 60's, with salt-and-pepper hair. I remember him looking down at me and shaking my hair as he chuckled while asking me that question.

I'm nine-and-a-half, I barked, arching my back to give the illusion of height. Just 30 seconds ago I was whining to my mom about not being able to go to the store alone.

Ahh, you're still so young. You're just a kid.

I'm not a kid. I'm almost 10!

My blood was curling. I remember my mom giving me that stare again. I was desperate to have my freedom. It was all I could think about day and night.

But the truth is that I was just a kid. Ten-years old is nothing, after all. You seldom have any freedom as a kid. And rightfully so. You can't quite look after yourself. And you certainly are far more naive to the world.

Yet, this concept is not just true in the real world. It also applies to the digital world. How often do we launch a site and expect it to rank right away? I've heard the story so many times that's it's become a running theme.

Robert, why can't I get my site to rank?

Well, for starters, it's new. Maybe not brand new, but in the digital world, it's not about your date of birth. Meaning, it doesn't matter when you bought your domain. What matters is what's happened since you've purchased it.

In the eyes of a search engine like Google, this is referred to as your Indexed Age. They care not about when you bought the domain. But, rather, when it was first indexed. And, of course, what's happened since then. Was content created? Did people link to it? And so on.

Many people think that they can just register a domain and expect to rank quickly. It just doesn't work that way. There's no level of trust. Imagine, as in the example of a new business, trying to get a loan from the bank with no personal guarantee.

Banks are weary of lending substantial sums of money unless there's some sort of track record. Google is very much the same. Google doesn't blindly trust like it once did. Today, you have to earn its trust. And that is not an easy feat.

Remember that trust takes time to build. But it can also be broken quickly. And once it's broken, it's hard, if not impossible, to go back. What does that mean exactly? If you attempt to employ shady tactics to help rank faster, you could suffer the wrath of Google.

Instead, it's slow and steady that will win the race. And

that takes time. The same rules apply to nearly every aspect of life. For example, good credit takes time to build. There needs to a long history of good credit management. The same thing applies in relationships. You don't start out completely trusting your spouse or partner. It happens over time.

RESEARCHING DOMAINS

The indexed age of a domain is a vital component to its ability to rank. Newer domains will have a harder time ranking than well-established, aged domains. We call them aged domains but really, we're referring to the *Indexed Age* of the domain.

That brings us to an important concept in the SEO world. When you're just starting out, it's harder to rank. But what if you could cut the line, so to speak and purchase an aged domain? Is it actually possible to do this? Well, the short answer is yes. But there's far more involved.

Google's algorithms are complex. But one thing is clear. A domain that's well-established and has a healthy link structure is one that can help to give you a solid platform. Yet, herein lies the problem. Simply purchasing a domain on its own doesn't quite cut it.

If you're really looking to supercharge your SEO efforts, you need to buy a domain with the content intact. Why? Because, in order to keep the validity of existing links to content on the site, you have to purchase the site outright. Not just the domain.

Obviously, this is more costly than just buying an aged domain on its own. But before we look at how to buy an entire site that you can use as your own, let's look at how you can buy a domain on its own. Because, let's face it, it's far less expensive to just buy the domain than the entire website.

Now, understand that there are websites dedicated to helping you buy both domains and entire sites. We'll look at both of these. But, first, let's look at how you can research a domain for purchase. To do this, we have to use a historical indexing tool called the, *Wayback Machine.*

You can find it by just Googling, *Wayback Machine,* or you can head to **web.archive.org** to access it. So what is this tool? Simply put, it can give you insight into the history of a domain, along with its level of traffic and even allow you to see snapshots of pages in the past.

It's a great tool, especially if you're interested in taking a walk down memory lane and seeing how sites like Apple, Amazon, Facebook and others looked many years ago. But, for our purposes, we'll use it to analyze any potential domains for sale.

So, how does this work? Well, for starters, if you have a domain (or you've had one in the past), you can simply enter it in. What you'll see in the results is a graphical depiction of the traffic along with snapshots of pages from the past.

#1 – Understand that Historical Content Matters

There is a treasure trove of information and data that comes along with this search, so you'll have to sift through it and review all the snapshots that are available. Why is this important? Well, if you're considering purchasing an aged domain, it should be a topical domain.

Meaning, you shouldn't buy a domain that is unrelated to your business or intended niche. Keep in mind that you're losing all the content when buying a domain on its own. Yet, topical relevance is important when building a domain.

If there were links created to content in the healthcare niche, but you buy the domain and use it for your garage floor refinishing business, it will add little to no value for you. It has to be somewhat relevant to your own business. That's why it's important to review topical information.

#2 – Review Any Potential Google Penalties

When you're researching domain ages using the Wayback Machine, another important thing to look out for are any sudden drops in traffic in the bar graph. These can indicate a couple of things that could impact your ability to rank.

The first could be that the domain suffered a Google

Penalty. Google Penalties can occur when a website breaks Google's rules. If it spams links, does sneaky redirects, or flagrantly breaks any other number of rules, it could suffer a penalty.

When a penalty occurs, you'll usually see a drastic drop in traffic. Meaning, the bar graph will take a nosedive. But that's not always why it happens. It could be that the domain changed hands as well. So you have to do a bit of digging.

The point is that you want to stay away from domains that have cyclical ups and downs of traffic in the bar graph. That usually indicates that its history is questionable. You want clean, one-owner domains, if possible. Think about it like buying a used car. The more previous owners, the more problems it's likely had.

#3 – Dive Deeper into the Reputation of the Domain

The reputation of the domain is a vital component of your research. The Wayback Machine can give you some insight into the history of the domain, but it won't tell you much about its reputation. Those traffic dips won't tell you about the reputation of the domain.

You have to use a couple of searches in conjunction with your Wayback Machine search. One of the searches involves getting info on the domain. This is called an "info" search. You can run this search by using the following search term: [info:domain.com].

This includes using the opening and closing brackets for the search and replacing domain.com with the name of the domain in question. This will give you insight into the type of business being run on the domain. Was it an ecommerce site, a blog or something else?

You can also gain some insight into pages that might link to the site, any similar webpages that might exist, and also cached, prior versions of the site as well. While the Wayback Machine does have some of this information, getting a bird's eye view in what Google sees is very relevant here.

The other type of search you can do to research the domain's reputation is to use another advanced search type on Google. When you search using **[link:domain.com]**, you can uncover any inbound links that may exist to the domain.

Understand that any of the existing links that are out there might not be linking to the homepage of the domain. They might be linking to other pages that no longer exist. That's not necessarily a good thing. This is where this strategy pales in comparison to buying a domain with the content intact.

Please note that if you do buy a domain itself, it's important to hunt down any links to non-existent content and disavow them.

USING SEMRUSH FOR RESEARCH

One tool that can give you deep insight into the reputation of a domain is called SEMRush. SEMRush is a great tool for any SEO. Not only can you research the reputation of a domain, you can also research the quality of its backlinks and many other facets.

However, SEMRush is not free. You'll need to pay for it. But it is money well spent. It can also help you track your keyword ranking on SERPs so I would highly recommend it. Still, please understand that SEMRush (or any other SEO tool for that matter) is just a tool.

They are not 100% accurate. Their entire business model is based on creating their own backbone of data mined from Google search results. That's a monumental effort. But SEMRush has their data down and it is accurate for the most part.

Plus, this gives you the ability to automatically track your efforts. Not to manually have to review your results. It will tell you about any new links created, links lost, and more, on a periodic basis. You can use these reports to track all of your SEO efforts.

- The things you can do with SEMRush are as follows:

- Run a technical audit of your domain

- Analyze the SEO strategy of your competitors

- Discover ideas for increasing organic traffic

- Research keyword ideas for your domain

- Gain deep insight to backlinks for any domain

- Track your keyword rankings on a daily basis

SEMRush is an invaluable tool and I would highly suggest using it to analyze any domain. This is true when researching a domain to purchase just as much as it is for analyzing an existing domain you already own. The insights you gain can help you to drastically improve your rank.

To begin your analysis, just head to SEMRush.com and enter in your domain name. It will prompt you to create your account at the next step. You can opt to start a trial or skip it. Entirely up to you. Either way, when you do analyze a domain, you can see loads of information about it.

This will help you to make an educated decision on any domain up for grabs. But it will also help you analyze any existing domain you have and audit for errors. Often, On-Page factors are quick and easy to fix and can result in a quick boost to your site's visibility.

For example, an analysis of Amazon.com yields a treasure trove of data. When you dig deep into the backlinks, which you can access from the left-hand menu, you can see the link growth. Obviously, you can also see things like the traffic trend, keywords trend and more.

PURCHASING DOMAINS AT AUCTION

Remember that age is more than a number to Google. And if you want to speed up the process of ranking for big keywords, it's important to have a domain with indexed age. However, the quick disclaimer is that doing this without content intact is not a guaranteed strategy.

It's risky. But if you're willing to take that risk, then you can certainly purchase an aged domain. While there are plenty of places you can hunt for aged domains, the best one I've found is to use GoDaddy Auctions. GoDaddy is a leader in domains, but most don't realize they also do auctions.

Now, domains come up for auction for many reasons. But the most common reason is that people simply forgot to renew them. This isn't always the case. Especially when we're talking about more popular domains. But, regardless, things do happen. People miss emails, renewals, or just have so much else going on in their lives.

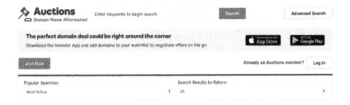

To begin the search, just head over to auctions.godaddy.com. When you get to the site, you'll notice that there's a search bar towards the top of the page. This is where you can enter keywords for your search. However, there's a more refined way for doing this.

At the top of the page, towards the right, you'll also notice a button that reads 'Advanced Search'. When you click that button, you'll see a popup with far more options that will help you find the right domain. It's vital because you get to select the specific criteria you require.

Here's precisely what you'll be searching for.

#1 – Domain Age

It's important to select a domain with some real age. If you're going to buy an aged domain, you might as well buy one that's properly aged. Now, remember, you're going after the indexed age. Although you can't see that on the GoDaddy search, you can on the Wayback Machine.

To select the age, just put in a minimum *Domain Age* on the advanced search. Use 5 years as the minimum and leave the maximum age blank. This will show you all the domains that were registered at least 5 years ago. This will give you initial data you can then further research.

#2 – Keywords

Another important element of your search are the keywords. What keywords do you want in your domain? While it's getting harder and harder to get shortened domains with competitive keywords, it's still possible to find longer domains with keyword association.

Make sure that you change the search type for the keywords to 'Contains' from 'Exact Match'. The 'Contains' option will show you all the domains that contain the keyword you're searching for, whereas the 'Exact Match' option would only search for domains with that exact keyword.

Clearly, the latter search would fail to produce any results. For example, if you put 'Dentist' as your keyword and picked 'Exact Match' the system would only search for dentist.com. Instead, if you choose 'Contains', it will search for any domain that contains the word dentist in it.

#3 – Domain Extensions

It's best to stick with top-level domains (TLDs) such as dot-com or dot-net where possible. TLDs like dot-com and dot-net domains will take priority over other non-TLDs in a Google search. Avoid country-specific TLDs like dot-us or dot-ca and others as well.

Most people don't realize this, but there are actually well over 1,000 TLDs that run the gamut. But these TLDs won't help you rank in SEO. Google simply favors the mainstays.

That doesn't mean it's impossible to rank without a dot-com or dot-net. It just means its far harder.

For the purposes of your search for an aged domain, select the dot-com option so that you only see those domains and you avoid the other extensions. You can also select dot-net, but dot-com will always take priority over the others, so you might as well just stick with that.

#4 – Attributes

For the attributes section, pick the 'Buy Now' option to search for domains that you can purchase straightaway without going through an auction. While an auction format is okay, it will lengthen the process. So there's no need to select it.

That's all you have to select here. You can play around with the other options or leave them blank and conduct your search. When you hit the 'Run Search' button, you'll get a list of available domains that you can purchase immediately.

However, your work doesn't end there. You'll need to conduct your due diligence on the domains. Remember to use the tools that we've already discussed to dig deep into the domain's history:

- Use the Wayback Machine

- Run a SEMRush audit and analyze the backlinks

- Use the advanced Google search options for info and links

Remember that this is an advanced strategy and that purchasing an aged domain doesn't guarantee you much. That's especially true when you don't purchase the content intact. However, if you do have a budget, you can use other options to buy entire websites with the content intact.

PURCHASING AGED WEBSITES

My absolute favorite strategy for cutting the proverbial line is to buy an aged website with the content intact. This works well because all existing links pointing to the site are still valid. All that's happening here is a transfer of ownership.

Keep in mind that this option is not cheap and if you're on a small budget, you'll likely get sticker shock at some of the prices. However, the beauty about this is that there are sites out there that allow you to buy entire aged websites that have positive cashflow.

Think about it like buying a rental property with existing tenants who are paying you rent every single month. It's profitable and puts money in your pocket. But you have to put a small lump sum down to purchase that rental property.

This strategy works well for SEO because you're buying an existing asset that's not only ranking in your industry, but also producing cashflow. And the best part is this. There are websites dedicated to helping people buy and sell sites like this.

One such website is called Flippa.com. They are one of the largest resources for buying and selling businesses. Yes, these are businesses you're buying here. Again, this option is not for everyone. But, if you truly want to skip the proverbial line, this is an excellent way to do it.

Remember, SEO takes time because trust is not built up overnight. But, if you were to take the reins of an existing business with pre-built trust, then you're not fighting tooth and nail for years to come just to rank. Again, this will work for some. Not for all.

When you get to the site, you'll notice a link that says 'Websites' at the top. You can use the submenus to search for a site by age. Pick the '5 years+' option for the best sites. There are plenty of sites here in all different niches and price ranges.

You can sort by lowest to highest price to see the most affordable sites. Or, you can simply look at the featured sites that show up in the default search. Those will be more expensive. Once you find a site that works, ensure you do your due diligence using the tools described earlier.

You'll want to use the Wayback Machine, SEMRush and advanced Google searches for any site that piques your interest. Plus, for existing sites, make sure you run a duplicate content search for each page with content. You can do that by using copyscape.com.

Copyscape.com will show you whether the content is original and if any of it is duplicated. It will also tell you where the duplicate source is from. Copyscape.com is not a free resource. But it is well worth it. You can use this as your last tool of due diligence when you're near a decision to purchase an existing site.

SECRET 6
CRAFTING DROOL-WORTHY CONTENT

In Elementary School, my 5th grade teacher, Mr. Parks, gave us an assignment in class. We had to write a story. It could be about anything. I remember sitting there beaming with happiness. I loved writing. Even back then. Although, I probably wasn't very good at it.

I still vividly remember that warm summer morning in class. Growing up in Long Island, I was used to the heat. But it was the humidity that was killer. I remember it so well because my shirt would stick to the back of my chair. And as I leaned forward, it would slowly peel off.

The windows were open, and the sound of a lawnmower hummed in the distance. The classroom looked out directly onto a large grassy field where you could catch a glimmer of the green John Deere mower as the sunlight bounced off it at just the right angle.

The smell of fresh-cut grass wafted in through the partially opened windows. I picked up my black ballpoint pen and started writing in the best cursive I could muster up. Instantly, I was transported into my story. The walls of the school melted away and it was just me at my desk, writing profusely.

It's funny how certain memories last in your mind. But the point of me telling you this story is to help illuminate an important fact. Content is king. No matter what anyone tells you, your content will make or break you. That doesn't mean content is the whole story (no pun intended). It's not. But it's a very large part of it.

Look, the truth is that without great content, no one will care about your site. No one will stop by and visit it if you don't engage and add value. But that doesn't mean you have to be a world-class writer to dominate search rankings. You don't. But you do have to be good at conveying ideas and telling stories.

Don't try to complicate things. The simpler your storytelling, the better. You don't want this to sound like a Doctoral Thesis. What you do want is to have descriptive content that helps tell a story and solve a problem. That's crucial to keep visitors engaged and reading.

One other concept I want to convey to you is this. Don't try to forcibly rank for a keyword. Meaning, don't try to hit a specific density of keywords in your content. Your goal is to ensure that the concepts conveyed are clearly about the topic of the post.

That means you shouldn't be obscure or go off on tangents. Be specific, but in a simple way. Explain the topic in deep detail and really go out of your way to help them solve the problem. This will help you get your content to rank.

Also, keep in mind that Google has multiple

technologies that allow it to understand both the search intention of the user and the content itself on a deeper level. For example, it can use a technology called Latent Semantic Indexing (LSI) to analyze the search term using a mathematical computation.

LSI allows Google to compare similar words and phrases at a more organic level. And while LSI was introduced way back in 2004, more recent technologies, such as RankBrain, introduced in late 2015, help analyze and determine the most relevant search results.

After RankBrain, Google introduced BERT in 2018. BERT stands for Bidirectional Encoder Representations from Transformers. The technology is based on NLP (Natural Language Processing), which was developed by Google.

BERT took cognitive understanding of search phrases to another level. This was a revolutionary leap forward, taking Google's NLP technology to another level with its ability to process entire words and phrases in the sentence rather than attempting to compare and contrast single words from one sentence to another.

This breakthrough happened because BERT can process search through transformers. Transformers are part of Google's neural network architecture, which is essentially a model that helps Google train its algorithms with far less computational power.

Today, with the combination of heavy machine learning, Google is able to accurately determine both the search side and the content side. It uses a variety of ranking signals to achieve this.

Combine that with state-of-the-art A.I. algorithms powered by their machine learning technologies, and you can see why Google search is so accurately.

HOW TO CRAFT GREAT CONTENT

Now that I've dished out a brief history lesson for you here, you hopefully have a better understanding of how Google's contextual search works. Even if you don't understand it at a mathematical level, it's important to understand this.

Google is now very good at analyzing both the intention and context of the search along with relevantly ranking all the search results in succession. I say that in order to stress the fact that there are no shortcuts when it comes to crafting expert content.

So, when it comes to your content, you have to go all out. If you're not confident in creating your own content, you can easily outsource. If you'd like my team to help you create your content, just go to outrankfast.com/content and we can assist.

When and if you do decide to create your own content,

here's how to craft it in a way that will rank you fast.

#1 – Create High Quality, Problem-Solving Content

First and foremost, it's important to understand this. Do not waste your time creating subpart content. It's a complete waste of your efforts. Instead, focus on creating the highest quality content that actually solves a persistent problem that your audience is experiencing.

Here's what this means. First, don't create thin content. Meaning, don't create short content. Avoid anything below 1,000 words. Why? Because, think about it this way. Can you really deep dive and help solve problems while also delivering massive value in a post that's 500 or 1,000 words?

You might think you can. But you can't. You need to go all out. Since most first-page results on Google hover in the range of 1,800-2,200 words, that means you need to have long-form content. And we're not talking about content that just babbles or dribbles on.

Get the picture? However, high-quality content also means other things. It means that you've properly checked it for spelling and grammatical errors. Imagine how difficult it is to convey real value if a post is littered with spelling or grammatical errors.

#2 – Make Sure Your Content is Well-Researched

You might be an expert about a topic. That's great. But there's a difference between writing content off the cuff and making sure it's well-researched. When you make a claim, include a link to a study or some other factual data to back it up.

In other words, you're citing your sources. People love to dig deep into the source of information and Google knows that. Plus, by citing sources, you're adding relevant external links, which is something else that Google really loves to see.

Make sure that whatever topic you're writing about, you're knowledgeable and experienced. Otherwise, it will be hard to deliver real value and help your customers solve their most pressing problems.

#3 – Create Keyword-Focused Content

There's a fine line between creating keyword-focused content and over-optimizing for a keyword. Most make the mistake of trying too hard to ensure their content has the right keyword density. That's not at all what you should be focusing on.

- Instead, make sure that your content is clearly about a particular keyword. You do this by doing things like:

- Placing the keyword near the start of the title

- Making sure your URL has the keyword near the start

- Using the keyword in the first and last paragraphs

- Utilizing headings that use the keyword or a variation of it

- Avoiding usage of irrelevant keywords

- Creating the content for users and not for search

engines

Keep in mind that Google wants you to create relevant, high quality content that's also simple to read. Specifically, Google says "Users enjoy content that is well written and easy to follow."

#4 – Make Your Content Engaging

Engagement is an important factor. Think about it this way. When you find a great piece of content, you spend the time necessary to read it, right? You likely also share it with others because it gave you so much value. And, by you sharing it, you're delivering that same value to the people you know.

Look, great content is engaging. It pulls you in and keeps you turning the proverbial pages. Google knows that. So, you should do your best to create the best type of content you can create. Literally, give away the farm to your readers.

It might sound counterintuitive. You might think, well if I tell them how to do everything, why would they buy anything from me? That's scarcity thinking. And what actually happens is far different. When you give way tremendous value, you actually become an authority.

People are willing to pay handsomely to others who are an authority in their field. When you offer these types of done-for-you services as a call-to-action in your content, it can transform your business. But to get there, you have to create great content that's also engaging.

#5 – Regularly Create Fresh Content

It's not just about creating longer, massive value posts. You also need a schedule where you can create fresh content regularly. Meaning, you should be pushing out content at least every week, if not more frequently. Now, I know what you're thinking. That sounds like a lot, right?

The truth is that if you want to compete with others, you have to put in real effort. There's just so many people vying for the same keywords that it's getting harder to rank, even for medium competition keywords. Create a schedule and outsource this task if you have to.

Just keep in mind that you'll need good writers who are well versed in optimizing content for a particular keyword. There's a science and an art to this. It's not just about the technicalities. Remember that. So invest the money to find someone skilled to help you.

#6 – Craft Content That Builds User Trust

Your goal is to create trust. That's done by being transparent, authentic and creating content that's unique. It's not done by duplicating content or using other shady measures to dupe a user. That will destroy trust. Not build it up.

However, when you cultivate trust, you can develop a reputation for being an expert in your field. This, in turn, creates authority. And authority is a foundational element for relevancy. Remember, Google's aim is to provide the most relevant search result first. Without authority, there can be no relevancy.

What else does it mean to craft content that builds user trust? This also means that you have to cite your sources, never copy someone else's work and claim it as your own, use a secure connection on your website, and more.

#7 – Create Long-Form, Factual Content

Google wants you to create long-form content. More specifically, as stated by the search giant themselves, there should be an "appropriate amount of content for your subject." While that might sound subjective, we've already seen how content in the range of 1,800-2,200 words tends to dominate the first page of Google's SERPs.

Plus, longer content tends to get shared more often. With so many studies to back this up, it's no wonder why this rule is so widely adopted. Knowing this, don't spend your time creating thin content. It's far harder to rank and largely a waste of your time.

#8 – Use Relevant Links Wisely

Google suggests that you should use your links wisely. Meaning, don't simply link to random sites. And keep in mind that your links pass your site's reputation (link juice) to other sites unless you use the *nofollow* attribute in the link.

That means, when you link to a site, part of the authority of your site gets passed on unless you tell Google not to convey it by using the *nofollow* attribute. However, that doesn't mean you should engage in excessive link sculpting.

Link sculpting is when you add attributes to all your links. That's not really the case here. You would only really sculpt links with attributes like *nofollow*, if you were linking to a site that you don't quite endorse.

Google also wants you to accurately describe the links. Avoid linking to external sites with phrases like "click here" or "learn more" and any other non-descriptive text. Internally, that's okay. But when linking to external sites, be descriptive about the nature of the link.

#9 – Make Your Content Mobile Friendly

Today, most of search happens on mobile devices. You likely know that. But some people still don't understand the importance of mobile-friendly content. Here's what you have to know. Make sure your content is designed to be responsive for mobile devices.

Some site owners make the mistake of not optimizing their content for mobile devices. In turn, their content suffers due to a lack of rank. There are ways to check the mobile friendliness of your content. Just head to https://search.google.com/test/mobile-friendly.

When you arrive, type in the URL of your content to see how well your page does. This is great for auditing any past content you may have created as well. Plus, you'll learn if your page is mobile friendly, and what, if anything, is wrong with it.

#10 – Optimize Images in Your Content

Google wants relevant images that are optimized. When you use an image, first off, you should have the rights to use it. For this, you can use any of the royalty-free image sites like Shutterstock.com or iStockPhoto.com, along with many others.

Also, you'll want to optimize and compress those

images. There are plugins for doing this for platforms like WordPress. In addition, you'll want to use an "alt" tag and an image name that is descriptive. Avoid using generic image names that make no sense.

Avoid doing things like creating extremely lengthy filenames or attempting to stuff keywords into the "alt" tag. That will raise red flags. Keep things natural and organic.

ON-PAGE SEO FACTORS

Anything that happens on the page itself is referred to as On-Page SEO. These are elements in your control. Of course, your own content is one of those elements in your control. What happens on the page itself is critical in determining your ability to rank.

Sure, you have to write great content. But that's not the entire picture. There's far more that you need to do. Things like site speed, mobile usability, AMP, and many others are all part of what makes up the user experience.

Google's main desire is to deliver a superb user experience to its customers. It knows that if it gives them the most relevant result quickly, they'll be satisfied. If they have to sift and search around for it after landing on non-relevant sites, they won't be quite happy.

But before getting too deep into the technical factors

that make up the foundation of good On-Page SEO, let's look at those that impact the actual content creation itself.

1. **Page Title** – The title of your page is one of the most important elements of your content. Stick with titles that are under 60 characters. However, the actual length of the title displayed can vary since some letters are wider than others and there's a 600-pixel container width. Use your primary keyword as close to the start of the title as possible.

2. **Meta Description** – Meta descriptions help to better explain your page's content to search engines. And don't confuse these for meta keywords. Those are no longer valid and are now deprecated. Keep your meta description to less than 160 characters in length.

3. **Headings** – Heading tags are an important part of On-Page SEO. You should be using your keyword (or an LSI variation of it) in your <h2> and <h3> tags. The <h1> tag is often reserved for the main heading at the top and is usually pulled from the title of the content in a system like WordPress.

4. **Page Structuring** – You have to properly structure your content using headings and paragraphs. This makes it easy to read and breaks up the page into a well-flowing piece. Think about old newspapers and how those larger articles were broken up into paragraphs and headings. Keep your paragraphs small (4 to 5 sentences long). And don't write run-on sentences.

5. **Crawlable Pages** – Your content must be easy to crawl. It also must be accessible to search engines.

Ensure that search engines can index your content, and you haven't mistakenly turned that off.

6. **Load Time** – Don't overburden your content with slow-loading images. Especially if you're using a shared hosting environment. Optimize your images and keep them to a minimum. Make sure your content loads quickly on mobile devices. Use Content Delivery Networks (CDNs) and a system like CloudFlare to increase DNS propagation.

7. **URL Structure** –Make sure you properly structure your URL to include the keyword. Make it simple and easy to read. Avoid very long URLs as they don't add to the user experience at all.

8. **Mobile Layout** – Make sure your content is responsive. Today, it's a mobile-first index. If your content doesn't properly load on mobile (and other) devices, it impacts the user experience. And anything that negatively impacts the user experience, will negatively impact your ability to rank.

Creating great content is not just about the technical structure of a page. While that's important, the larger focus must be on creating something of real value. We're talking about Massive Value Posts (MVPs) that can take 10 to 15 hours or more to craft.

However, writing just one MVP won't do it for you. You have to be consistent and constantly create MVPs that solve problems for your audience. By now, you should know what those problems are. But there's something else that you should do as well.

In marketing, curiosity is a very important element that

attracts users to a piece of content. We use curiosity to drive clicks. I'm not talking about clickbait. I'm talking about compelling content that draws users in, but then keeps them engaged.

Obviously, this happens with the page title. It's important to interweave curiosity into your title to keep people curious. When they're curious, they'll be more likely to click on your content. And, Google does track clickthrough rates. Meaning, even if you rank lower, but your post gets clicked on often, and keeps people engaged, you will move up the ranks over time.

So how do you use curiosity in your headline? For example, instead of "Fear is the Number One Factor that Makes Dogs Bite You", you can say "This is the Number One Factor that Makes Dogs Bite You". Can you see the difference? It's a simple change but creates curiosity.

Another example would be "Five Telltale Signs to Know She's into You." Can you see how this stirs curiosity? Rather than telling them upfront, you have to create curiosity. This is part of the art in the process of creating content. It's not just about the technical factors.

REVERSE-ENGINEERING CONTENT

Tony Robbins says that success leaves clues. And if you want to succeed, find someone who's already successful and model what they're doing. Note, he says to *model* and not to copy. So what does that mean in the world of SEO?

Brian Dean, a popular SEO blogger who runs a website called backlinko.com, talks about a strategy called the Skyscraper Technique. In the Skyscraper Technique, you're discovering great content and stacking on 20 stories to the building. Hence the term, *skyscraper*.

Meaning, you're adding to content that's already getting significant traction. It's already ranking high, has lots of backlinks, and is generating lots of social shares. Essentially, it's already vetted out and deemed relevant by Google and its users.

This is the epitome of modeling someone who is already

successful. To do this, all you have to do is search for some of the most competitive search terms in your industry. What content is ranking number one? Once you find that piece of content, review it and consume it.

Then, ask yourself this question. How can I make this content better? The goal here is to add to the content and improve it. Please understand that this is not about duplicating content. You have to give it your own unique spin while making it far superior.

There are 3 overall things that you want to do when utilizing the Skyscraper Technique.

Step #1 – Find High Quality, Linkable Content

The first step here is to locate content you can model. This is simple. Again, just conduct a Google search for the most competitive search terms in your industry. Then, click on the number one spot on Google. This is the content you'll model your content from.

To analyze the link profile of the content, all you have to do is use a system like SEMRush.com or Ahrefs.com. These will give you a complete backlink profile of that particular URL. You'll need this for step number three.

Step #2 – Create Far Superior Content

Next, you'll need to create content that's better. No, scratch that. You have to create content that's far superior. I'm talking about going all out here. This is not just about adding to the content. You have to actually make it better.

Remember, you're dealing with a highly competitive

field here. Especially when we're talking about very competitive search terms, you truly have to put in a great deal of effort. There are millions of people vying for the same search term after all.

So how do you do it? First, consider making the content more thorough. Meaning, you should go deeper on the topic. Being hyper-focused on the details here really helps. You'll need meticulous attention to detail to really make this work.

Also, consider bringing the content up to date if it's outdated. Some of the time, you'll discover outdated content that ranks well on Google. If that's the case, refreshing it, while also making it more thorough will certainly help you rank that content.

Lastly, consider upgrading the design. You can hire a graphic designer on Upwork or Fiverr to create nifty graphics for your post that should help increase the user experience. However, be careful not to add too many images that might bog down the load time.

Step #3 – Start Your Outreach Services

Finally, take the link profile you analyzed in step 1 and sort them by domain rank (DR) to find the most popular sites linking to the old content in question. Then, reach out to those sites and offer your site as an alternative link. Explain that it's better, more thorough, has a better design, and so on.

This will seem tedious at best. You can a hire an outreach service to do this if you'd like, but it's far more effective to do it on your own. This will take time and a lot of emails. You'll likely struggle with non-responsive individuals as well.

However, you have to keep at it. There are lots of links to popular content, so that will give you lots of opportunities for backlinks. Plus, you should stay persistent and keep emailing those who don't respond. But do it once per week at most. Stay persistent and committed and you will succeed with this strategy.

ROBERT KANAAT

GOOGLE'S WEBMASTER GUIDELINES

Now that we've covered an overview of how content can
and should be constructed, let's look specifically at Google's
Webmaster Guidelines. You can find these guidelines online
by going to:

https://support.google.com/webmasters/answer/35769

Google breaks these down into general guidelines and
quality guidelines. The general guidelines cover things like
helping Google to find your pages, helping them to
understand your pages and in helping users to use your
pages.

General Guidelines

To help Google find your pages, there are a few rules you

140

should adhere to. Here's what they suggest doing:

- Every page on your website should be reachable by a link from another reachable page. Meaning, you shouldn't have pages that are simply unreachable via link from elsewhere on your site. That link should either be a textual link or an image link using the "alt" tag.

- Make sure to create a sitemap file. You'll need both an XML version of this for Google, and a readable file for human visitors.

- Avoid having too many outbound links on a page. Google says to limit this to a few thousand, but even that is excessive. Keep your linking to a minimum and ensure they're highly relevant.

- Make sure your web server supports the If-Modified-Since HTTP header, which indicates changes in your content since the last time Google crawled your site.

- Manage crawling on your site by using robots.txt. Most people won't have to worry about this, but the main concern is crawling infinite sections of your site such as the search. Google offers a robots.txt testing tool that you can access by visiting: https://www.google.com/webmasters/tools/robots-testing-tool

To help Google understand your pages, there are a few rules you should adhere to. Here's what they suggest doing:

- Be clear and descriptive about your content and

build information-rich pieces that deliver real value.

- Understand the keywords users use to find your content and make sure to use those words.

- Use detailed <title> tags and "alt" attributes that are specific and accurately describe the content.

- Have a clear hierarchy in your site to allow users to easily find the information they're searching for.

- When using a CMS like WordPress or any other, make sure that you allow search engines to crawl your pages. There is usually a setting that you can turn on or off. For example, WordPress has a checkbox in the settings > reading section of the system that says, "Discourage search engines from indexing this site."

- When using images, Google suggests making them relevant to the context of the post and to optimize the placement of it, placing the most important image at the top of the page. They should also be optimized for speed, good quality, and use descriptive titles, filenames and "alt" tags.

- If your site uses session IDs or other parameters in the URL, you should allow Google to crawl your site without those requirements.

- Use rel="nofollow" and rel="sponsored" for any advertisements on your site so that search engines don't follow those links.

To help visitors use your pages, there are a few rules you should adhere to. Here's what they suggest doing:

- Avoid using images and opt to use text. If you use images, make sure that you add a descriptive "alt" attribute.

- Make sure that all your links go to live webpages and not 404 or dead pages.

- Optimize your page for fast load times. You can use the Page Speed Insights tool provided by Google at: https://developers.google.com/speed/pagespeed/insights/

- Ensure that you create a responsive design that's friendly on all viewports such as desktops, tablets and mobile devices.

- Optimize your site to work properly in different browsers.

- Utilize HTTPS to secure your site.

- Test usability of your content with a screen-reader.

Quality Guidelines

Google breaks their quality guidelines into two parts. It has its basic principles and also more specific guidelines.

Basic principles

- Create pages for humans. Not for search engines.

- Don't be deceptive.

- Ask yourself the question, "Does this help my users" when considering any SEO tactic.

- Make your site engaging and create valuable content.

Specific Guidelines

- Avoid creating any type of content that's generated automatically.

- Don't participate in any type of link schemes. Google defines link schemes as anything intended to manipulate PageRank. This includes, but is not limited to, buying or selling links, exchanging links, large-scale article marketing, using automated services to generate links, and requiring links as part of a contract or terms of service.

- Don't create duplicate content.

- Don't cloak webpages. Cloaking involves showing humans different pages than search engines.

- Avoid sneaky redirects.

- Don't create hidden text or links.

- Don't use doorway pages, which are sites that are intended to rank for specific keywords.

- Don't scrape content from other sites.

- Don't do any sort of affiliate marketing without creating real value.

- Don't use irrelevant keywords on your webpages.

- Don't create pages intended to phish or install viruses.

- Don't abuse structured markup.

- Don't send automated queries to Google.

- Monitor your site for hacking.

- Remove (and prevent) any sort of user-generated spam, such as in blog comments, forum posts, and others.

ROBERT KANAAT

SECRET 7
RANKING SECRETS

To understand the secrets behind ranking, you have to understand how Google's search algorithms work. We've covered a lot of ground, but let's look at the search side of the equation. What Google really wants is to display the most relevant results first, right?

So, what is relevancy at the end of the day? With so many search results, how does Google actually determine who's displayed first, second, third, tenth, one-hundredth and so on? At the core of this is trust. We've already seen that.

But how do you get Google to trust you? And how do you do it fast? To explain this, let's take a deeper look at the Google search algorithm. Keep in mind that there are many algorithms working together. It's not just one. But all of the algorithms combined are looking for 5 key factors:

1. The meaning (intention) of the search phrase or query

2. The relevance of the webpage itself

146

3. Quality of the content on the webpage

4. The user experience of the webpage

5. The context and settings of the search

#1 – The meaning (intention) of the search phrase or query

Search intention is important. In Secret #3, we discussed the four different forms of intent in a search. If you'll recall, those are informational, transactional, comparison and navigational. Google's algorithms work hard to analyze a search for intention first.

Google has worked tirelessly to create language models to understand what, specifically, you are looking for. Although seemingly simple to human minds like ours, algorithms have to process the words and phrases using a number of mathematical models.

Beyond the synonyms, nouns, adjectives, pronouns and other words you might find in a search, algorithms must also be able to interpret things like spelling mistakes and even slang. The algorithms must also work to understand whether this is a specific search or something broader.

It also has to look for other words that might indicate the type of search you're attempting to make. If the word "reviews" or "opening hours" exists, the system interprets this as a search for business information. Other words like "pictures" interprets this as an image search.

There are also freshness algorithms at play here that work to deliver fresh content. For example, if you're looking for "basketball scores", the algorithm understands that you're looking for the latest scores on games being played now or very recently.

This information is important because in order to rank for a particular keyword, you have to understand the intent of the searcher. When you can get into the mind of the searcher, you can deliver the right content at the right time.

For example, if you run a graphic design business, it's important to not only understand who your customer is, but what information they're searching for. The biggest mistake that business owners make is not understanding how the sales cycle relates to content on their website.

Meaning that most people who search for something are not ready to buy right away. Business owners get frustrated because, not only do they lack traffic, but the traffic that they do receive fails to convert. Content and ranking in search is great, but you also have to understand how to create a customer.

#2 – The relevance of the webpage itself

Relevancy involves many factors working together. Not just on the webpage, but also at the domain level. At its core, relevancy requires trust. The more trust there is, the more chances your webpage will be deemed relevant.

However, it only starts there. To be deemed relevant for a particular search, the first obvious component necessary is a relevant keyword. The question is this. Is your webpage relevant to the keyword searched and the individual searching for it?

But that's not all. Even if your keywords appear in the title, URL, headings and body text, there are numerous other factors at play. Google calls these factors "aggregated and anonymized interaction data," which they use to assess the relevancy of your webpage.

That's just a fancy way of referring to the historical clickthrough rates and engagement of your content. Meaning, do people click on your search result? And if they do click on it, how engaged are they? Do they stick around and read it, or leave fairly quickly?

This comes back to the art of SEO rather than the science of it. If your title creates some curiosity (without being considered clickbait), and people click on it even though it's not the top search result, that's a good thing. And, when they click on it, if they stick around and consume it, and potentially even visit other pages on your site, that's an even better thing.

#3 – Quality of the content on the webpage

The quality of the content is crucial. Google uses a system called E-A-T to determine this. It stands for Expertise, Authoritativeness and Trustworthiness. This is determined by not just the content itself, but also the creator, and the website the content is found on.

The expertise of the creator of the content is a crucial factor. How much of an expert is the content creator? This is important. And it's also why your name should appear as the author of the content. Google has quality raters that actually research content and its creators.

How much authority a creator has is important as well. Remember, authority comes from other websites that Google trusts. Meaning, if you already have mentions in other popular media sites or high-ranking domains, that's a good thing.

However, this can also work inversely. If you have

negative reviews or a bad reputation, then it can harm your authority. However, the authoritativeness is not just about the main content, but also about the domain in general.

For the trustworthiness, the same applies. It's not just about the trustworthiness of the content, but also of the entire website. How much trust does it have? There needs to be an ample amount of E-A-T in order to send a high-quality signal.

Ensure that you have your website information up to date. Google needs to know information about the site and its creator. This includes putting your name, address, and even phone number in some cases. This is especially true if you are selling anything on the site.

To Google, there are four characteristics of a high-quality page:

1. High level of E-A-T

2. An ample amount of valuable, high-quality content, which includes having a "descriptive or helpful title."

3. Information related to the website owner.

4. Positive site reputation and content creator reputation (if different).

#4 – The user experience of the webpage

Your site must be easy to use if you're serious about having it rank. This means that it should have a clear hierarchy and be simple to navigate. It should not confuse those who visit or make it difficult to find the right information.

This means it should also load correctly in different browsers and devices. It also means that there should be an acute attention paid to the page speed itself. Is it slow loading or is it lightning fast? Or maybe somewhere in between.

There are many tools, some of which we already discussed, to help you with your site's page speed. This should be a priority. And not something you do later on. Use Google's Page Speed Insights tool or webpagetest.org to test your page speeds, and work on improving them.

The user experience also has to do with things like excessive ads that appear above the website fold. That's where the website gets cut off before scrolling. Also, any annoying popups or redirects might severely harm your chance of ranking.

#5 – The context and settings of the search

If you're in Portland, Oregon and you search for *best tax accountant*, Google displays local search results. Similarly, if you search for *football scores* in London, England, you'll get soccer scores and not NFL scores. Your country and location are important to the search results as they add relevancy to certain queries.

This is also applicable when Google is determining the context of the search. Meaning, if you were to search for *Barcelona*, but yesterday you searched for *Barcelona vs. Manchester*, Google will assume you're searching for the soccer team and not the actual city in Spain.

In addition, Google will use your geographic location to help determine relevancy when you search for things like *best pediatricians* or *Italian restaurants*. Google is guessing you're searching for those things near you and not around the country or world, unless you specify that.

THE ART OF LINK BUILDING

Every single week, without fail, I receive dozens of requests from random strangers who are eagerly looking for a backlink on a piece of content I've written. It's tiring, to say the least. And begging randomly for backlinks doesn't work.

However, please understand this. Link building is an art form. You have to do it the right way. Not by begging content creators for links to your new app or website. That doesn't ever work. Especially if you haven't first developed a relationship with that creator.

What does work is this. You must be willing to deliver real value to a content creator. How, you might ask? There are many ways. What I'm going to cover here are the ways that have worked best for me. Now, part of this does involve some outreach.

So if you're not comfortable with outreach, get

comfortable. Why? Because it's part and parcel to link building. You can't expect links to materialize out of thin air. It doesn't quite work like that. If you can't, find an outreach service to help you.

However, before you reach out to anyone, it's important to wield the right strategy. You can't link-build by begging for links. Especially not on quality sites. You have to develop and nurture relationships, while also delivering real value.

So how do you deliver real value to someone? We've already discussed the Dream 100 strategy. There's always that option. But in a pure link-building scenario, here's how you do it. First, you should have already identified the top bloggers and sites in your industry.

Who are they? Make a list. Now, what you don't want here are direct competitors. They're not likely to give you links. What you want are complementary sites. For example, if you sell health insurance, you'd target popular content sites in the health niche with high domain authority.

You can use a tool like Ahrefs.com or SEMRush.com to identify domain authority (or domain rank). It's a quick and simple search to do this. But the best way to find these sites is to search for competitive search terms that your potential customers are already searching for.

If you sell health insurance, what searches would spark interest in getting a new health insurance policy? Maybe a relocation to the area. Or, maybe changing jobs or getting married. You really have to put thought into this, and even poll your existing customers and just ask them.

Other ways are by using a tool like Ahrefs.com or SEMRush.com to analyze your direct competitors. What search terms are they ranking for? What are the top terms companies in your niche are ranking for? You can easily analyze this simply by inputting the domain name.

Either way, understand that it will be a steep climb in the beginning. Your focus first should be to create rock-solid content that delivers massive value. Without it, you'll have nothing to link to. Take the time to really create high-quality posts first and foremost.

Once that's in place, analyze popular content that's already ranking on Google. Search for dead links in the content that you could recreate, but better. This is somewhat similar to Brian Dean's Skyscraper Technique from Backlinko.com.

However, with this approach, you're looking for popular content with dead links. Dead (404) links are a huge no-no in SEO. But even the most popular sites can't keep up with every link that turns into a 404 at some point. Your job, then, is to find those links.

For example, to continue on the example of health insurance, let's just say I search for best health insurance. That's a pretty competitive search term. Plus, your geographic location will likely play a role in this search. One of the first results for this search is from a popular site called Investopedia.com.

When we take that link and insert it into Ahrefs.com, we can analyze whether there are any broken links.

Buying Private Health Insurance ⓘ How to use
www.investopedia.com/articles/pf/08/private-health-insurance.asp ▾

Ahrefs Rank	UR	DR	Backlinks	Referring domains	Organic keywords	Organic traffic	Traffic value
598	37	91	909 -95	146	4.8K -175	25.5K -515	$127K
			Recent 1.2K	Recent 164	PPC 0		PPC $0
			Historical 1.90K	Historical 261			

Backlinks profile   Organic search   Paid search

When we analyze the webpage that ranks at the top of the search results, we see that it has 909 backlinks. Once you click on the backlinks, you can dig deeper. On the left-hand menu, scroll down to find the section called Outgoing Links and click on *Broken Links*.

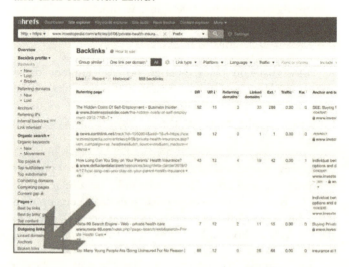

If there are no broken links, you'll get a notification that says there are no broken links. However, if broken links do exist, this is where your opportunity awaits. Your job is to hunt down those broken links and work on replacing it with better content.

How, you might ask, if the link is broken can you replace the content? Our little friend, the Wayback Machine, has the answer to that. Simply input the broken link into the Wayback Machine and have a look at the historical content that you find.

Next, your job is to create equally great content. It's easier said than done. You can't copy here. Remember that. All you can do is model the content. If it was a list of the 5 vital factors that impact the type of health insurance you purchase, then create something better.

Maybe you do an article on the 7 vital factors that impact the type of health insurance you buy. Does that make sense? It doesn't necessarily have to be a numbered list. The point here is to model the general style of the content. This is important for when you notify the site admin about the broken link.

You see, regularly swapping out links is frowned upon by Google. It indicates that you're potentially selling links. Not always. But it's certainly a flag. However, when the link breaks because the site linked to is no longer online or the piece of content moved, that's a different story.

The broken link negatively impacts that site. So, they are far more apt to fix the issue. This is a way you can deliver value to a site owner. This will take some legwork and research, along with some outreach. But it is worth your while.

CREATING LINKABLE ASSETS

Years ago, when I first launched WanderlustWorker.com, I worked tirelessly to create content about things like habit building and goal setting. And as I built out great content, I often scoured the web for resources. The aim was to find scientific research I could use to back up my claims.

Interestingly enough, I stumbled on a "new" study conducted by a site called Statistic Brain. That study claimed that 8% of people achieve their long-term goals. I say new because, the following year, when I found the study again and clicked on it, it had been updated for the current year.

Now, when I say updated, I mean that the year was changed. Nothing else. So it looked like a brand new study. Again. But the interesting thing about this was that it ranked #1 on Google for a long time when searching for *goal setting study*.

I linked often to that study because it backed up the claims I was making in my articles. The claims were that goals set on New Year's Eve don't pan out and that most people quit. The study actually broke down how many weeks people lasted with their New Year's Eve goals.

Why is this important to you? Effectively, what Statistic Brain did, was that they created a linkable asset. Scientific studies or research is an absolutely terrific way of doing this. And when you do, it beckons links from all over the place.

I often link to studies that I find to back up my writing. As we've already seen, Google loves when you cite sources. But what about becoming the actual source that people cite? That's when it really dawned on me and I thought, *oh wow, if you just create these studies, people will link to you.*

This is hyper-effective in garnering high-quality links. Mind you, this is not clickbait. No, no, no. This is far from it. This is high quality, scientific research. But I do use the term "scientific" here somewhat loosely. Because, after all, you're probably not a scientist.

Many sites publish in-depth studies to help solicit links. NerdWallet is one of those sites that often publishes studies on things like household debt, student loans, and other finance studies. Why? Because, they're the most powerful link magnets you can create.

So, here's how this works:

1. Find a topic in your industry you can create a study about

2. Create a series of questions that you can use for your study

3. Use a large sample size to research your data

4. Create your "report" as an online study and aptly optimize the title and content around it

5. Hire a graphic designer to help with the graphical elements

You can also take this a step further and offer it as a downloadable PDF with extra details. This way, you can even use this as a lead magnet. This helps you effectively kill two birds with one stone. Sure, this will take a lot of effort on your part. So don't expect it to be simple.

In the SEO world, nothing is quite simple. That much should be pretty obvious by now. However, the amount of work this takes pales in comparison to constantly researching broken links, creating high-quality content, and then hoping the website owner will replace those broken link with your new resource.

VIDEO MARKETING

It's no secret that video continues to surge online. And it's not just YouTube. Video is now becoming commonplace throughout social media sites. In fact, TikTok, an all-video social media platform, experienced an exponential rise due to its unique approach to social media with video.

The truth is that video will become more and more important online. Of course, YouTube is the second largest search engine behind Google. And that should tell you something. You need to have a video marketing strategy to supercharge your SEO.

Now, the problem with this is that most people don't like to be on camera. I get that. However, the beauty about YouTube is that you don't have to. You can literally make videos and do simple voiceovers without actually appearing on film.

There are numerous channels out there that are crushing it by using this strategy. However, you don't even need to do this yourself. There are, in fact, services out there that you can hire to make these videos for you. All you need to do is provide the transcript and layout.

Okay, so there is some effort involved. However, video is where you want to be. If you don't have a video marketing strategy, it's important that you create one. Plus, Google is doing more to incorporate video into search through video snippets.

You've likely seen video snippets before in search. The beauty is that Google pre-selects the snippet that is most relevant to the query. This way, you don't have to watch the entire video. All you're doing is watching the most relevant part of it as it pertains to your query.

In order to qualify for a video snippet, you should transcribe all your videos and give them clear sections. When you have distinct sections, you can cordon off your content so that it might appear in a snippet. And, don't rely on YouTube's automatic transcription. Sometimes it's not completely accurate.

Have each of your videos transcribed and upload them directly to the video. It's also important to have great cover photos and keyword-rich titles that create curiosity without being considered clickbait. Be careful about how much curiosity you attempt to create.

LOCAL SEARCH MARKETING

Every business online understands the power of presence. Traffic, leads and sales all follow once you appear relevantly. But that's not just true for larger, more competitive keywords. It's also true for local search marketing as well. It's far simpler to rank locally, in fact, than it is to rank globally.

So what is local search marketing, really? It's simple. It involves a service from the search giant itself called, Google My Business (GMB). You've likely already heard of this before. But if you haven't, now is the time to utilize this service.

This enables you to setup a free business profile so that you can easily connect with potential customers online. This is simply another avenue for getting business. It helps you to promote your business, not only on Google search, but also on Google Maps.

This allows you to display things like your phone number, store hours, website address, street address and more. Allowing customers to interact with your business like this is another cog in the wheel of commerce. It will also help you collect Google reviews for your business as well.

In addition, GMB will allow you to post special offers from your business, and even add photos. This will help you to highlight what's important to customers as they first interact with your business. Of course, this is really applicable mostly for consumer-facing businesses.

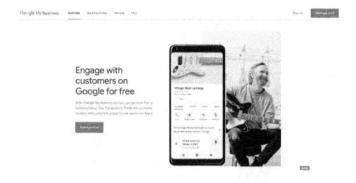

The process for setting this up is largely self-explanatory. Just head to google.com/business to get started. You'll need your Google account to login or manage your existing business. But you can also add your business through this process as well.

You'll have to go through a verification process in order to set this up. But, keep in mind, that the link from GMB is simply another powerful backlink to your website. So, if nothing else, it will give you just a little bit of extra link juice.

ROBERT KANAAT

SECRET 8
GOOGLE'S RANKING FACTORS

Want to dominate Google's search engine and crush your competition? Well, it's not easy. You've likely already gotten wind of that. There's a lot of information to absorb and understand. But the fundamentals should be clear by now.

Google has multiple algorithms working together to ensure that you get the most relevant search result fast. That's done by building trust over time. Okay, that much is clear. But what are all the factors involved? If you're the type who likes to drill down into the details, this next part is for you.

While Google's Webmaster Guidelines paint part of the picture, it's not the whole story. There's a lot involved. And in the following list, you'll find a comprehensive take on ranking today. Much of this list is credited to Brian Dean of backlinko.com, so a big shoutout to him.

Here, what you'll find are over 200 ranking factors that go into Google's current ranking algorithms. Hopefully, it'll illuminate what to do and what not to do when it comes to Google's search. Now, understand that some of these

166

signals are weaker than others.

No one knows the exact strength of each of these factors. Nor do they know specifically which factors are in-play, so to speak, at any given moment. Why? Because, Google's algorithms are constantly evolving and morphing.

So, don't take the following list as hard and fast rules. Instead, use your best judgment to determine if it's something you should adhere by or not. Most of this comes from highly relevant sources, and even public data released by the search giant itself.

So, what are these illustrious 200+ ranking factors included in the latest generation of Google's search algorithms? They're split up into two separate categories:

1. **On-Page Optimization** – Anything to do with the domain or webpage itself. On-Page Optimization (sometimes referred to as On-Page SEO) is more in your control than Off-Page Optimization.

2. **Off-Page Optimization** – This refers to anything that happens away from the webpage. Off-Page Optimization (also called Off-Page SEO) is harder to control or keep tabs on. This includes things like content marketing, link-building, reviews and so on.

Of the two categories, we have far more control over what happens on the page, and far less control over what happens off the page. That doesn't mean that we can't influence the off-page factors, it just means we have far less sway over them.

For example, when speaking about links generated, editorial content, reviews left, or any other off-page factor, we can influence these, but at the end of the day, since they're happening away from the page that we have control over, we can't command what actually happens there.

Of the two categories, there are seven separate sub-categories when it comes to the 200+ ranking factors that go into Google's algorithm. The full list goes as follows:

1. On-Page Optimization

    a.   Content Factors

        i. **Quality**

            1. Expertise? – Is the content from an expert in their field. Does the individual creating the content have enough expertise to share the information?

            2. Page speed? – What's the page speed score? You can use Google's Page Speed Insights to generate your score for mobile and desktop. A good score will be anything above 80 for both mobile and desktop.

            3. Keyword-centric? – Is the webpage dedicated to a single keyword? Does it appear relevantly in the title, heading tags and content?

            4. Keyword in first paragraph? – Does the primary keyword appear in the first paragraph?

            5. Keyword in last paragraph? – Does the primary keyword appear in the last paragraph?

            6. Duplicate content? – Has the content been duplicated from another source? You can use

copyscape.com to check for duplicate content, especially if you're hiring others to write your content.

7. Image optimization? – Are the images optimized and being lazy-loaded? Is the main image a high-quality image that you have the rights to use?

8. Image ALT tag keywords present? – Does the main image incorporate the primary keyword in its "alt" tag?

9. Image name keywords present? – Does the main image use the primary keyword in its name?

10. Number of outbound links? – Are there too many outbound links? Be careful not to have too many outbound links.

11. Quality of outbound links? – Are all the outbound links on the page relevant and high in quality?

12. Theme of outbound links? – Does the theme of the outbound links match the page's theme? It's possible that Google could be using the page's theme of the outbound link as a relevancy signal.

13. Grammar and spelling? – Is grammar and spelling spot-on? Use Grammarly.com to give a quick and thorough check of the content before publication. Too many spelling and grammar mistakes could indicate low-quality content.

14. Syndicated content? – Is the content on the

page original or was it copied from another source? If it was copied, was it sourced? Syndicated content won't rank as high as original, unique content.

15. Audio & video on page? – Relevancy signals indicate that high-quality audio, video, or other multimedia on the page increases the quality of the content.

16. Number of internal links to page on site? – Signifying the importance of a page on a particular site, multiple internal links to the same page can be an increased relevancy signal.

17. Quality of internal links to page on site? – Pages on your site with high PageRank and other positive relevancy signals have a greater impact linking to any other particular page on your site.

18. Number of outbound links in your content? How many outbound links are present in the content? Are these nofollow links or dofollow links? Although nofollow links are better in terms of SEO, too many nofollow links might also signify excessive link curating.

19. Internal link anchor text? – Are there internal links in your content pointing to other content on your site? What anchor text is being used? Although this is a relevancy signal, it's relatively weak, but still one that Google uses to understand the bigger picture of your content.

20. Internal link title attribution? – Do you have
    title tags in your internal links on your
    content? If so, what keywords are being used
    in them? Are they reinforcing the content's
    primary keyword or pointing to a secondary
    page that helps to reinforce the existing
    content?

21. Broken links on page? – An excessive
    number of broken links can indicate that a
    site has either been abandoned or put
    together carelessly. Broken links also
    decrease the user's experience. And, anything
    that decreases the user's experience,
    decreases relevancy.

22. Affiliate links present? – Are affiliate links
    present? Google doesn't like affiliate links but
    will tolerate them as long as they're not
    excessive and your policies do indicate that
    some of your links will generate you an
    income if they purchase from them.

23. Hidden affiliate links? – Quite possibly one
    of the worst things that you can do. If you're
    hiding your affiliate links, then you're
    cloaking your content. And, by now, you
    should know that this is absolutely not
    tolerated by Google. Expect a drop in rank if
    you do this.

24. PageRank? – What's the PageRank of the
    page? Has the page built some authority?
    Pages with a higher PageRank will have a
    greater chance of appearing randomly in
    Google's SERPs if all other factors are equal.

25. Host domain PageRank? – What's the

PageRank of the host domain? This is a moderate relevancy signal. Remember the importance of PageRank to authority sites? If the host domain has a high PageRank, this will help the underlying content on any page of that site.

26. Indexed age of the page? – How old is the page? When was it first published? Freshness counts for some topics, but Google also looks to content's overall age as a relevancy signal.

27. YouTube video? – Does the page include a YouTube video? Multimedia on the page, especially videos that reinforce the content, is a moderate relevancy signal to Google.

28. Linking to bad link neighborhoods? – Do you have links going out to bad link neighborhoods? This could be a weak relevancy signal and an indication of low-quality content.

29. Over optimized page content? – Have you gone overboard with optimizing for your keyword? Is your keyword density too high, making the content sound unnatural or forced? This will result in a small penalty.

30. Auto-generated content? – Have you auto-generated your content with a software system to spin or re-rewrite something that resulted in poor quality content? Stay away from these frowned-upon practices.

ii. **Research**

1. Research sources cited? – Have you cited

sources or Websites with information from research studies or other quotes and references that you've provided?

2. <u>Statistical information provided?</u> – Have you provided statistics and figures to backup any claims that you've made in your writing?

iii. **Length**

1. <u>Is the content over 1,000 words in length?</u> – Well-written content over 1,000 words will rank higher than shorter content.

2. <u>Is the content over 2,000 words in length?</u> – Content over 2,000 words but under 2,500 words generally tends to rank the highest on Google's SERPs.

iv. **Engagement**

1. <u>Time spent on page?</u> – How much time are visitors spending reading your page? How engaged are they?

2. <u>Bounce rate?</u> – What percentage of visitors leaves after visiting your page from Google's SERPs? High bounce rate could indicate that the visitor's question was answered as long as the visitor spent enough time reading your content.

3. <u>Exit rate?</u> – Are visitors moving to other pages on your site after visiting? If so, what other pages, and what are the exit rates from those pages?

v. **Freshness**

1. <u>Recent content or updated content?</u> – How fresh is the content? We know that age matters, and that older content generally tends to rank higher than newer content. However, older content could and should be updated with new information when and if it becomes available.

2. <u>Magnitude of content updates?</u> – If content was recently updated, what's the magnitude of the update? Was it just a few words changed here and there, or did sections and entire pages get overhauls?

3. <u>Historical updates to page?</u> – What are the historical updates to the page? How many times has the page been updated and what types of updates occurred?

vi. **Thinness**

1. <u>Low word count?</u> – Thinness is a penalty. If you keep your content's word count very low, you can expect to rank low or nowhere at all on Google's SERPs. If the content is thin, consider adding a YouTube video to help boost the quality and counteract the thinness. But, overall, you should consider always keeping your word count above 1,000 words.

2. <u>Low quality?</u> – What's the reading level of the content? Is the quality low? Was this just thrown together quickly, or was it well written and well thought out?

vii. **Number of Ads**

1. <u>Ads above the fold?</u> – How many ads exist above the Website's fold? Does this decrease

the user's experience?

2. <u>Ads below the fold?</u> – How many ads exist below the fold and where do they exist? Do the ads disrupt the user's experience?

b. HTML & CSS Factors

i. **Page Title**

1. <u>Keywords in title?</u> – Are the primary keywords used in the page's title?

2. <u>Keywords starting title?</u> – Do the primary keywords start the title of the page? This is a strong relevancy signal.

3. <u>LSI keywords in title?</u> – Are LSI keywords used in the page title?

4. <u>LSI keywords starting title?</u> – Do the LSI keywords start the page's title?

ii. **META Description**

1. <u>Keywords in META description?</u> – Does your primary keyword exist in the META description? This is a moderate relevancy signal.

2. <u>Keywords starting META description?</u> – This is a weak relevancy signal, but also might be a sign of over-optimization.

3. <u>LSI keywords in META description?</u> Do LSI keywords exist in the META description? This is a moderate relevancy signal.

4. <u>LSI keywords staring the META description?</u> Another relevancy signal but could be

stronger than the primary keyword starting the META description, since it looks more organic in nature.

5. Spammy META tag? – Do you have a spammy, keyword-stuffed META description? Is it difficult to read?

iii. **Page Headers**

1. Keywords in H1 tag? – Is the page's primary keyword in the H1 tag? In some systems like WordPress, the H1 tag is also used as the title of the page.

2. Keywords starting H1 tag? – Do the keywords start the H1 tag? This is a moderate to strong relevancy signal.

3. LSI keywords in H1 tag? – Do the LSI keywords exist in the H1 tag?

4. Keywords in H2 or H3 tags? – Does the primary keyword exist in the H2 or H3 tags?

5. Keywords starting H2 or H3 tags? – Does the primary keyword start the H2 or H3 tags? This might be good, but it also might be a sign of over-optimization. Be wary when implementing this.

6. LSI keywords in H2 or H3 tags? – Do the LSI keywords exist in the H2 or H3 tags? This could be a positive relevancy signal as it moves away from over-optimization.

7. LSI keywords starting H2 or H3 tags? – Do the LSI keywords start the H2 or H3 tags? Another positive relevancy signal as it also

moves away from over-optimization.

iv. Page Structure

1. Layout quality? – Is the overall page easy to read and follow? How about the navigation? Can you easily move from one section of the site to another?

2. Sectioned and easily readable content? – Has the page been broken down into sections with easily readable content?

3. Usage of lists and bullet points? – Are lists being used with bullet points or numbers? This is a moderate relevancy signal.

4. WordPress tags? – Are WordPress tags being used? This is a weak relevancy signal and only allows relating one page or a group of pages to others.

5. Priority of page in sitemap? – How high up is the page in the sitemap hierarchy?

v. Keyword Stuffing

1. Over usage of keywords? – Have you overused your keywords? This could result in a moderate to severe Google penalty.

vi. Hidden Text

1. Invisible text with CSS? – Have you hidden text anywhere on the page using CSS? This could result in a penalty.

2. Text placed a far distance below page end? – Have you tried to hide text by placing it far

away from the page's visible elements, such as far off down the page past where the visitor would generally stop reading? This could result in a penalty.

c. Website Architecture

  i. **Website & Crawlability**

   1. Number of pages? – How many pages exist on the site? Are they properly organized and easily reachable from any other page on the site?

   2. Sitemap present? – Is an HTML and XML sitemap present?

   3. Site uptime? – Does the site suffer from elongated down times or have other hosting problems that could have an effect on the user's experience?

   4. SSL certificate? – Is this a secure site using SSL encryption with a certificate from a trusted provider? SSL sites are an absolute requirement today for ranking on Google's SERPs.

   5. Terms of service & privacy pages? – Do you have terms of service and privacy pages on your Website? This could be a weak relevancy signal.

   6. Breadcrumb navigation? – Another weak relevancy signal to move through a stack of related pages.

   7. Easy to navigate? – Overall, is the site easy to navigate? Can we move from one section to

the other without much difficulty?

8. Usage of Google Analytics? – Although not documented, many believe that the usage of Google Analytics is a weak relevancy signal.

9. Usage of Google Search Console? – Although not documented, many believe that the usage of Google Search Console is a weak relevancy signal.

ii. **Duplicate Content**

1. Duplicate text throughout site? – Do your pages have repetitive text in them? Are you repeating certain paragraphs, sentences, or keywords in the same manner on your pages? This could result in a decrease in relevancy.

2. Duplicate META content? – Do you have duplicate META content on your pages? Are you using the same META description on multiple pages? This could result in a decrease in relevancy.

iii. **Site Speed**

1. HTML load time? – How quickly does the HTML load on your page? Slow pages will decrease the user experience.

2. Google Chrome load speed? – How quickly does your site load in Google Chrome?

iv. **Page URLs**

1. Canonical URL? – Are you using canonical URLs that are easy to read and understand, and accurately depict the content of the page?

2. Keyword in URL? – Is your page's primary keyword present in the URL?

3. Keyword at start of URL? – Does your page's primary keyword start the URL? This could be a moderate to strong relevancy signal.

4. LSI keyword in URL? – Are LSI keywords present in the page's URL?

5. LSI keyword start of URL? – Does your URL begin with one of your LSI keywords?

6. URL length? – Is your URL too long, or just the right length? Stay from very elongated URLs and from stuffing keywords unnaturally in them.

7. URL path? – Does the URL path help to reinforce the relevancy of the page?

8. URL string? – Is there a URL string that's incorporating too many variables? Google won't read beyond the first variable in a URL string, after the question mark for example.

v. **Mobile-Friendliness**

1. Is site mobile friendly? – Is your site mobile friendly? Can visitors easily navigate and read the site on a mobile browser or do the elements get confusing?

2. Is site mobile optimized? – Are the touch elements too close to one another? Is the page optimized for mobile?

2. Off-Page Optimization

a. Links

i. **Link Quality**

1. Domain age – How old is the domain that's linking to you? This is a strong relevancy signal as it's also an underlying factor in authority. Older domains will have built more authority over time.

2. IP diversification – How diverse are the IP addresses for the links coming to your site? Keeping all your links to only a group of IP addresses doesn't indicate authority. Google wants to see global authority.

3. Link text – What words are being used in the link text? Does the link seem natural and organic? Or, does it seem like the same link text is being used repeatedly?

4. Keyword in link text? – Is the page keyword being used in the off-page link text? This is a relevancy signal, but it can be abused.

5. LSI keyword in link text? – Is the LSI keyword being used in the link? This could indicate higher relevancy when coming from the right type of content, comment, or post.

6. .EDU links? .GOV links? – Depending upon the PageRank and content of these links, it's a widely held notion that they deliver more link juice.

7. Linking page authority? – How much authority has the linking page built? Keep in mind, this isn't the authority of the domain, but the page where the link is coming from.

A link from a page with more authority will be an increased relevancy signal.

8. Linking page relevancy? – How relevant is the linking page to your page? Does the content there have some tie-in to the content on your page? This is another moderate relevancy signal.

9. Word count on linking page? – How many words are there on the page containing the content that's linking to you? Is the link coming from within that content or from a sidebar or footer?

10. Quality of linking content? – Remember, high quality content that links back to your high quality content is a great relevancy signal.

11. Linking domain relevancy? – How much relevancy does the top-level domain on the linking page have to your content?

12. Linking domain authority? – How much authority does the top-level domain have? How many links are there going to the domain? SEO Quake sheds some light on this for us as we've already seen.

13. Links from competitors? – Do you have links from competitors? This could be a relevancy signal.

14. Social shares of referring links? – How many people have shared the link of the page that's linking to your content?

15. Guest post link? – Guest posts can be a good

thing, but not always. Google released a statement way back in 2017 warning against using guest posts to distribute links. Be careful if implementing this strategy as it might backfire depending on the content and the domain the guest post is distributed on.

16. Bad link neighborhood? – Do the links come from a neighborhood filled with bad links? For example, link farms or any other site that might have been given a Google penalty might negatively affect your relevancy.

17. Nofollow or Dofollow link? – Google doesn't follow "nofollow" links. Matt Cutts once stated, "In general, we don't follow them." Try to get links without this attribute, or the "dofollow" attribute for increased relevancy.

18. Link type diversity? – Is there diversity in this link from previous links? Are all the links coming from the same place or do they have some diversity? Google likes to see a wide range of sites linking in and not just the same sites over and over again.

19. Sponsored link? – Links coming from sponsored content won't have as much link juice as those coming from natural, organic, or editorial content.

20. 'Contextual link? – Do the links come from empty pages or profile pages with no other data? These could reduce the relevancy signal and link juice of those links.

21. Excessive 301 redirects? – Has the linking

page moved from another domain or URL?
If there are excessive 301 redirects from the
linking page, this could be a decreased
relevancy signal.

22. Anchor text of link? – How natural is the
anchor text in the link? Is it placed organically
within content or does it seem forced,
spammy, or unnatural?

23. Title tag of link? – Is the link using a title tag
to help reinforce the relevancy of it? Title tags
in links are similar to the ALT tags used in
images.

24. Location of link on page? Footer, sidebar or
within page content? – Footer and sidebar
links have less relevancy than links placed
organically within content.

25. Link comes from a poor review or a
recommendation? – Google can determine
whether the link is coming from negative
content or positive content about the page
being linked to.

26. Links from top resource pages? – Top
resource pages on the Web are links that have
enormous authority and generally come from
elongated list posts.

27. Link from authority site? – Is the link coming
from an authority site domain?

28. Wikipedia links? – Is the link coming from
Wikipedia? Wikipedia is a site with an
enormous level of trust built with Google,
and links from them hold more relevancy and
carry much more link juice than standard

links.

29. Link age? – How old is the link? How long has the link been around for? The older the link, the more relevancy it tends to extend.

30. Links from real sites? – Is the link coming from a site with little traffic that was just setup in an attempt to build more links? Or, is the link coming from a real site with real traffic and user interaction? Google can differentiate between the two.

31. Natural link? – Is the link a natural and organic link, or is it some form of paid or advertised link? Is it coming from natural and organic content?

32. Reciprocal link? – Is this just a reciprocal link? These hold less relevancy. For example, if you were to exchange links with someone, it won't hold as much importance as a natural link.

33. Links from 301 page? – Are the links coming from a page that's recently moved to a new URL or domain? These could have decreased relevancy.

ii. Link Numbers

1. Separate referring root domains? – How many links are coming from different domains?

2. Excessive low-quality links? – Too many low-quality links from low PageRank or spoof pages will decrease your relevancy.

iii. **Link Velocity**

1. Positive link velocity? – Are the number of links increasing from month to month?

2. Negative link velocity? – Are the number of links decreasing from month to month?

3. Unnatural link velocity? – Are there too many links coming in? For example, did the site go from 100 links to 10,000 links in one month? This can result in a severe Google penalty.

iv. **Paid Links**

1. Excessive paid links? – Is the site purchasing links, and doing so excessively? Is there a high ratio of paid to natural links happening?

v. **Spammy Links**

1. Spammy link text? – Is the link within the text spammy or unnatural? Is the link coming from a page with no content in an effort to simply build relevancy?

2. Poor quality links? – Are the links poor quality? Do they come from real content or empty pages? Do the pages contain spammy text?

b. Trust Factors

i. **Content**

1. Useful content? – How useful is the content that's linking to your page?

2. Content provides value? – How much value does the content provide that's linking to

your page?

3. Content provides unique insights? – Does the content linking to you provide unique insights?

4. Contact us page? – Is there a contact us page present with information? Google uses this to determine real sites from fake sites.

ii. Authority

1. Link selling? – Is the page that's linking to you selling links to others? How much authority does the page have? How many other natural and organic links are going to the page linking to you?

2. Google Sandbox? – Has the page in question suffered from a penalty? Is the page in Google's Sandbox?

iii. Age

1. When was the domain first registered? – Older domains tend to have more authority and trust. A weak relevancy signal looks at the date the domain was first registered.

2. When was the domain first indexed? – A stronger relevancy signal comes from the date that the domain was first indexed by Google. Has it been two or more years or is it brand new?

3. When does the domain expire? – A Google patent reveals that the domain expiration date is a relevancy signal. Most spammy sites are only registered for one year in advance

whereas "serious" domains are registered for years in advance.

iv. **Domain**

1. Keywords in domain? – Does the page's primary keyword exist in the domain? This isn't as strong of a relevancy signal as it was in the past.

2. Keywords in subdomain? – Do the page's keywords exist in the subdomain?

3. Keywords as first word in domain? – Is the keyword the first word in the domain or does it start the domain?

4. Exact match domain (EMD)? – Does the page's primary keyword match the domain name exactly? Google is wary of these so-called doorway pages using domains intended to rank for a particular keyword.

5. Domain history – Has the domain switched ownership multiple times or has the traffic fallen off in peaks, or has there been a steady and natural buildup in the domain over time?

6. Public or private registration? – Private registrations could be an indication that the domain owner has something to hide.

7. Country top-level domain extension (TLD)? – Is this a top-level domain such as .US or .CA?

8. Whois ownership specific data – Who owns the domain name? Is it a real business?

9. Parked domain? – Is this just a parked domain?

10. Domain Trustworthiness? – How trustworthy is the domain linking to you? Have they built up trust with Google over time? Have they had any penalties?

v. **Piracy**

1. DMCA complaints? – Have there been DMCA complaints about the domain or page linking to you?

2. IP Address flagged as SPAM? – Has the IP address of the linking domain been flagged for SPAM or blacklisted?

vi. **Relevancy**

1. Domain diversity on SERPs? – The Bigfoot algorithm update helped to diversify domains on SERPs so that a single search wasn't wielding too many results from the same domain.

2. Transactional searches for shopping-related queries? – Searches that are using micro-data can now appear for shopping related queries. How relevant is your search when it comes to this?

3. Big brand relevancy? – Big brands tend to appear at the top of SERPs for certain short-tail keywords. This was part of the Vince algorithm update.

4. Brand name search text? – Does the search text involve a brand name? This is a moderate

relevancy signal.

5. Brands with higher likes and shares on Facebook and Twitter? – Does the brand have a high number of likes and shares on Facebook and Twitter?

6. Image results? – Images can come before certain SERP listings on popular image searches.

7. Easter egg results? – These are moderate hoaxes. For example, if you search with the word "askew" or "tilt," that will change the orientation of results. Similarly, Google might deliver games in its SERPs from time to time as well.

8. Single-site results from brands with multiple SERP listings? – If the search is for a brand-oriented keyword, Google's SERPs might bring up many listings from the same domain.

9. Real business? – Is this a real business? Is it a legitimate operation? This has an effect on relevancy.

10. Verified brick-and-mortar location? – Has the physical location been verified through a service like Google My Business?

11. Tax-paying business? – Is the business a tax paying business?

12. Google algorithm update penalties? – Has the domain suffered any Google algorithm update penalties?

13. Manual penalties? – Has the domain suffered from manual Google penalties?

c. Social

i. **Social Reputation**

1. Site reputation? – What type of social reputation does the site have? Has it been reviewed or rated?

2. Social media votes? – Are there social media votes for the site?

3. Social signal relevancy? – How relevant are the social signals that are pointing to the site?

4. Site-level social signals? – Does the site have strong social signals? How many people shared and liked it?

ii. **Online Reviews**

1. User reviews? – Are there positive user reviews for the site?

iii. **Social Media Share**

1. Number of Tweets? – How many Tweets does the site or page have?

2. Authority of Tweet users? – What's the authority of those tweeting? Do they have a large and active real following?

3. Number of Facebook shares? – How many Facebook shares does the site or page have?

4. Number of Facebook likes? – How many Facebook likes does the site's page have?

5. Authority of Facebook user accounts? – What's the authority of the Facebook user accounts that like and share the page?

6. Number of Pinterest Pins? – How many Pinterest Pins does the page have? How many does the site have in total to the domain?

7. Website has a Twitter profile with followers? – Does the Website have a Twitter profile? Are there followers?

8. Website has a Facebook profile with fans? – Is there a Facebook page setup for the company with real fans?

9. Official LinkedIn page for company? – Does the company have a LinkedIn page?

10. Employees listed on LinkedIn pages?

11. News media mentions of site?

d. User-Specific

i. **Country or Region**

1. Geo targeting search? – Is there any country or geographic targeting that needs to be considered with the search? Things like top-level domains and region-specific data come into focus.

ii. **City or Locality**

1. Locally applicable search? – Does the keyword apply to locally applicable search? How relevant is it for a local search?

iii. **History**

1. <u>Click-through-rate (CTR) for a keyword in searches where you relevantly appear in the results</u> – What's the CTR for that particular keyword search?

2. <u>Click-through-rate for all keywords in searches where you relevantly appear in the results</u> – What's the CTR for all searches related to your site?

3. <u>Bounce rate of users visiting your site?</u> – Are they leaving the page without visiting other pages? Did they find the answer they were searching for or did they not like what they read? This is used in conjunction with time spent on the page.

4. <u>Exit rate of users visiting your site?</u> – What's the exit rate of users visiting that page from a SERP? Is the exit rate high or low? Are they visiting other pages?

5. <u>High direct traffic?</u> – Is there a high level of direct traffic to the page or domain?

6. <u>High repeat traffic?</u> – Are users going back to certain links again and again? These sites are considered as higher quality by Google.

7. <u>Blocked websites?</u> – A signal used in Google's algorithm penalties, blocked sites were part of the user-experience. However, this is no longer part of Chrome.

8. <u>Google Toolbar data?</u> – Information is collected from Google's toolbar for user-specific searches. How much time are they

spending on a page, and what other user-specific search factors are involved with that search?

9. Time spent on site? – A greater number would indicate higher quality of content. This data could then be used in subsequent searches.

10. User's browsing history? – What sites has the user visited in the past? Would that increase the relevancy of the page in question?

iv. **Social**

1. Large number of comments and user interaction? – Are there a large number of comments and user interaction about the shared links?

2. Safe search? – Does the user have safe search enabled? And does your site have any kind of profanity or adult content that would stop it from appearing.

THANK YOU

Thank you so much for taking the time to read this book. I've put a lot of care to ensure that the information is accurate and up to date. Hopefully, it's been insightful for you. If you've received from value from it, I'd invite you to please leave a review with your thoughts and comments.

Also, please make sure that you join the Facebook Group. That's where you can ask me questions directly and get my input on anything related to SEO. You can find it located at the following link:

https://www.facebook.com/groups/seotrainingacademy/

www.ingramcontent.com/pod-product-compliance
Lightning Source LLC
LaVergne TN
LVHW041211050326
832903LV00021B/570